ARLOTT
In Conversation
with
MIKE
BREARLEY

ARLOTT

In Conversation
with

MIKE BREARLEY

John Arlott   Mike Brearley

Hodder & Stoughton
in association with Channel Four Television

London   Sydney   Auckland   Toronto

This book is based on the Channel Four Television series *Arlott in Conversation with Mike Brearley*, produced by Derek Brandon for Cheerleader Productions Limited.

Designed by Jeremy Dixon

ACKNOWLEDGMENTS

'Passing the Graveyard' reproduced by kind permission of Secker and Warburg Limited from *Poetical Works of Andrew Young* edited by Edward Lowbury and Alison Young

'To John Berry Hobbs on his Seventieth Birthday' reproduced by kind permission of John Murray Publishers Limited from *Jack Hobbs: Profile of "The Master"* by John Arlott

British Library Cataloguing in Publication Data

Arlott, John
  Arlott in conversation with Mike Brearley.
  1. Arlott, John 2. Sportscasters – Great
  Britain – Biography 3. Sportwriters –
  Great Britain – Biography 4. Cricket –
  Great Britain – Biography
  I. Title II. Brearley, Mike III. Channel
  Four Television Company
  791.44'5   GV742.42.A7

  ISBN 0-340-37641-4

John Arlott, a man of many parts, generous to a fault, generous in deed and in thought. He is a lover of cricket and cricketers, but well aware of the dictum 'what do they know of cricket who only cricket know'.

When I was asked to come to Alderney to spend some days getting John to talk about his life and his interests and his pleasures, of course I was delighted. I should like to announce from the start my allegiance to him: he is a man who has always fascinated me; he has sometimes been overkind to me; he has always been entertaining, always been aware and passionate. You won't see Robin Day interviewing the Prime Minister, but I hope you will share in a conversation that was much enjoyed by both of us.

MIKE BREARLEY

Alderney, one of the Channel Isles

Mike Brearley *John, here we are in Alderney. I wonder, what made you choose to come and live here when you decided to retire?*

John Arlott I have been coming here for a long time, first of all by accident. A man named Bill Tayleur, a neighbour in Highgate, introduced me to the island in 1951 and I always wanted to come here and retire. There are several things: first of all the tempo is superb, secondly it's extremely quiet and thirdly, I think it's most important, people of the island let you live your own life. It's completely peaceful as far as I am concerned. Nobody worries me, nobody bores me and I can live alone and not see anyone except my wife or my family for a week and then go to a party or have some people in to dinner, something like that. I find it the absolutely perfect existence and also of course it's very good for my bronchitic chest because the air is so clear.

But you must, you have a fascination for islands, haven't you?

Yes, I have. Now it's very funny, I have had friends here who say they find islands claustrophobic. I find them terribly secure, I almost like being deserted. But I have you know, I

7

suppose all my life, had this island thing, ever since as a kid I used to be taken to the Isle of Wight for summer holidays. And you see when it became difficult to come back here to Alderney for holidays, I used to go to Scilly, which I found immensely attractive and I almost retired there. I felt I needed an island.

But then you know at almost a moment's hint I came back here and brought Pat and Robert who had never been before and Tim[1] who hadn't been for eleven years and we all just decided that this was the place for the 'old man' to retire to. I am sure the boys were glad of the chance to get me off the mainland and be rid of me, though they come over here fairly often – they're all right. So it all flooded back over me how much I liked this place and it hasn't disappointed me in the least.

You showed me last time I was here a fort that is a sort of peninsula off the island and the causeway gets flooded, and you told me you would have liked to buy it.

It gets cut off completely. You tell me why – what makes a man love islands, want to live on an island, almost the smaller the better?

I don't know. What makes you want to?

I don't know. I wonder, do I feel more secure? Is it because when I was young I was entranced by *Robinson Crusoe* and *Treasure Island*? There must be something about an island.

Security also – that makes me think of something else. I thought you said to me once that there were no policemen on Alderney, but that's not true.

Oh no, no, there are three and they all turned up at the airport just before you got in yesterday. I wondered if it was a reception committee, but I think they only wanted a coffee.

But I mean a place where there is absolutely, or virtually, no crime at all and where life is peaceful no one's going to bonk you on the head.

No. There is no vandalism. I mean somebody did bowl a boulder through the jeweller's window after the jeweller decided not to insure, but they have found all that. They got

[1] John Arlott's wife and two sons

John Arlott at home in Alderney

all the jewellery back, rather more than the jeweller had estimated the value of it. But no, there is no crime, it is extremely peaceful. It is an uneconomic and non-viable island, of course, and expensive in many ways to live in, but so easy to live in. I've never known anything quite so restful.

Funnily enough, I suppose it sounds contradictory, it's simply easy to work here, largely because nobody interrupts you. People think twice about telephoning because it isn't on the mainland. Yes, I doubted, I wondered for a little when we first came, but there is no doubt at all now.

I suppose another thing about Alderney is everyone knowing each other. It's small enough.

I know; everybody knows everybody else.

There must be a fair bit of gossip, mustn't there?

Oh, terrible gossip, yes, Lord yes. You say good morning to somebody of the opposite sex, and that's enough for somebody to think you are having an affair! That's a bit hard, but clear air, clear sea, good restful tempo, splendid tempo coming from a main road in Alresford, it's been . . . pretty peaceful.

Mike Brearley at home

John, we touched on security. One of your first jobs, I think your second job probably, was being a policeman and then becoming a detective. Why did you do that and what was so interesting in that to you?

First of all my father wanted me to have a secure job. We were poor. I grew up in the slump and the desperate thing that my father wanted was that I should never be out of work. So first of all I went into the local government office and then into the mental health service as a doctor's clerk – all pensionable jobs, you see – and then into the police force which was also pensionable.

Southampton police had about the best club cricket side in England, so I thought if I could combine that with security I would be doing fairly well. I wouldn't say, though, that I was ever a particularly good policeman or a particularly good cricketer, but it seemed to me a way of growing up. It seemed to me that offices were petty and small-minded and that the police force would be bigger and more virile and more manly – I was wrong. It could be very small-minded in those days; I don't know if it is now. There is greater freedom, there is not the appalling backbreaking discipline of the chaser sergeants and the chaser points you know, driving you round the beat at three to three and a half miles an hour as some of those old sadists used to do.

But I suppose it was a way of life that brought you into contact with people in a way that perhaps it wouldn't do so much today.

Yes it did, and that was perhaps the most valuable part of it all. The other thing is, of course, that it is a hardening process. I don't say it makes you into a bully, but it removes physical fear which is very useful indeed and if somebody says, 'I'll clock you,' you're not frightened. I mean, it may be that he is going to clock you, maybe he is going to knock you down, maybe he is going to produce a great big black eye, but you have had a black eye before – boxing and things like this – you are not physically frightened which I think is a good thing.

The young John Arlott in 1932

You reckon that being a policeman helped you.

Oh, I know it did. Yes, it makes you altogether more self-reliant and less fearful and more generally secure in outlook, I think.

Would you be a policeman now? If you were starting again now, do you reckon that you would still feel a sympathy with the police force?

I have talked to my sons about this and said I thought they could do much, much worse than join, say, as a police cadet on the police force for a year or two to pick up a certain amount of self-reliance and nous and general appreciation of the way people in general behave.

And before that the mental health job. Was that an interest or was it merely a branch of the civil service?

I was a doctor's clerk in a mental hospital and I was working with patients most of the time, and doctors and diet clerks, and I was frequently on the wards. In your teens you see, that is a very morbid experience.

Again it teaches you a terrible amount about life and about people and the fact that the people they call insane are in fact ordinary people with just one little kink, one little twist, one little oddity. I wouldn't have missed that. I wouldn't have missed either, but I wouldn't want to have spent as long as I did in either really.

You were there for four years?

Four years doctoring and eleven years in the police force.

One of the reasons I was interested in your starting off working in a mental hospital, is that you were young, weren't you, in your teens?

Yes, I was sixteen. Sixteen and a bit.

I can imagine you having a very good rapport.

I did read – I didn't need to – I did read the mental nursing books and I still remember the definitions and how important it is that insanity be considered as – what is it? – 'such disability of the leading functions, thought, feeling or will, as should disable a person from thinking the thoughts, feeling the feelings, or performing the duty of that branch of society to which he belongs'.

I think that is fairly accurate. I haven't looked at it now for over fifty years, but what I am sure of is that it does relate to the branch of society to which you belong. If a tramp comes along and sits down on the kerb and pulls a sandwich out of his pocket, eats and spits in the gutter, all right. But if the Archbishop of Canterbury did it, he would be certified.

So you did, I think, come to learn there a much greater tolerance perhaps than you might have found anywhere else and so often, you see, there are therapies; you do see people improve. People improve just by doing a very humble job in a mental hospital, checking the accounts or something like that because they used to work in an office, and suddenly the strain seems to go out of them.

There is a lot to be said for the whole idea of the social therapy or media therapy, of giving people, coming back to the idea of independence, giving people within an institution the greatest possible freedom that you can.

But at the same time protection.

Oh yes, protection from others and from things that they might do themselves. But within that, within those restraints, to have as much say as possible, I think.

And you see it used to be explained to me sometimes. I would say that such and such a patient seems to me perfectly all right. Yes he is, they would reply, but if he went out into the world he would instantly go to the wall. So long as he is in here he is safe, secure; his laundry is done, his food is there, his cocoa is there, his bed is there, he will be all right. And this so often proved true.

The biggest problem of course is that the institution itself tends to create that dependency so you are in a sort of Catch 22, so that the longer they stay in the harder it is.

True not only of mental hospitals but many other places. True of the army, true of the navy, that many people get in there and find themselves protected within the cocoon and don't want to get out of it.

Even true of cricket teams, I think, and of sportsmen, that they feel safe. I do remember that when I first played for Middlesex there was a feeling that unless you had played twenty times for England and played for about ten years, you should keep your opinions to yourself, at least about tactics. And I think that is something that has changed, partly because I helped to change it, but also because of society changing, I mean that people are much freer to say what they feel.

Yes, this is true, the tyranny of the senior pros has disappeared, but that was a fantastic tyranny.

I can remember as quite a small boy, dear old Sam Pothecary – I wasn't a boy, but a fairly young man – dear old Sam Pothecary taking me to the team supper in a boarding-house off Russell Square with the Hampshire team. And Sam was talking to me, waxing very enthusiastic and all of a sudden there was a horrible hush because he was the junior member of the side and he was raising his voice. It was a hush of

John Arlott as a young BBC producer in 1947

disapproval; he realised what had happened, he looked round and there was old Phil Mead looking down from the head of the table. He didn't say anything to Sam, he just turned to Alec Kennedy and said, 'Yes, you were saying, Alec'. It was almost like being a child.

Did Hampshire do this? I believe Middlesex used to do it when they were away; they would have a long table – this was before the war – they would have a long table and the senior pro would dish out the food and hand it down to the juniors at the far end.

Oh, they did. They used to say at Hampshire it was just impossible for a young player to get in. There were six elderly professionals of immense status and the boys used to flicker around the edges of it all.

I don't know how accurate my facts are, but fairly accurate, I think. Jim Bailey, slow left arm and a fair batsman too, once took 6 for 16, and was near about the top of the first-class averages in June yet only played one more match to the end of the season. He was a pro on the staff. He went away of course and didn't come back for two or three years. He went to the Lancashire League.

But the tyranny of the old pros over the junior pros was terrifying and so, mind you, was the tyranny of some of the amateur captains over the professionals. But it was a strange feudal world such as couldn't happen, wouldn't be allowed now.

I think we are back again with the security in it, too, the security of knowing your place even if it's at the bottom, and knowing also that if you stayed there for fifteen years you would work your way up the table.

Yes, and the lack of change. Things change now at a vast rate.

I remember talking to my mother not long before she died and she was saying that when she got married there was no radio, no television, no internal combustion engine, no motor-car, no aircraft and she lived to look at television and see a man land on the moon. All right, it's trite, I know, but it does show just what has happened to us and how difficult, understandably difficult, it is for many people to adjust. I don't know about you, you may master computers; I stand in utter awe of computers, yet I go round to my friends' houses and their 10-year-old's putting computers together with DIY kits and, you know, one never knows whether to stay an 'old square' or try to live up to it.

Well, the thing that you said has been most important to you is human relationships and they are still going to be just as important. You can have as many computers as you like, but you have still got to have people running them with their emotional problems and their emotional depths and variety.

And it's the only real standard, of course. All right, I have said I have retired to a place, but you don't really retire to a place, you retire to people. I have got three or four friends here, and my friends that come over from the mainland, people like you, Leo Harrison, Geoffrey Moorhouse and so on, and just to see them is enough and that leaves me extremely happy.

I go to the mainland for two reasons: extreme social obligation, like if my aunt or my cousin should be ill, or a Masters Club lunch, Cricketers' Association, the Alresford Lunch, perhaps the Old Boys' dinner, that's the lot. Or for extreme financial inducement which doesn't happen very often. But now I have retired to the island I try to stay on it as much as I can. A retirement – you won't have to face it for a long time – is a conscious withdrawal. I always remember somebody saying once to Patsy Hendren,[2] 'Why are you retiring, Patsy?'

He said, 'Why do you say that?'

They said, 'What do you mean?'

He said, 'I am not going to wait until you say why not.'

I think if you have got the courage to retire, and understandably many people haven't, you have got to accept that it is no good making perpetual farewell appearances and doing a Dame Nellie Melba. You have got to go.

As you have already said, you're writing and you're occasionally induced to talk to people like me, or go to the mainland, and occasionally your voice is heard on the television in the advertisements, so you are not fully retired, you are leading what many people would call an extremely active working life.

In some ways I am possibly working harder than I have ever worked before, but you see I had to leave cricket commentary for two reasons. First of all I wasn't getting the spontaneous freshness and the originality that I once did. You know when you are losing your faculties and in your mid-sixties you are not as bright as you were, not as quick, not as rapid, your

[2] Middlesex and England

17

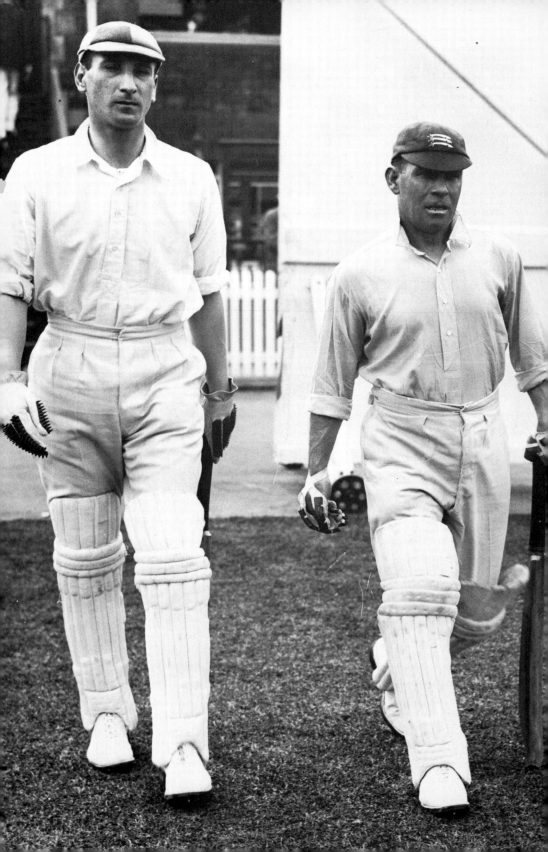

speed of reaction is not so good. The other thing was that I could do my share of the commentary and write a cricket report, but when I had to go out at twenty to seven at the end of the last day with 240 miles to go home and then a match at Taunton the next day, the sheer hassle of it became intolerable.

I think it begins to pall as a player. I found touring especially so, and doing it not only in the summer but all winter, I didn't have so much mental energy for it and it's more physically tiring as well.

What about now, Mike, now that you have retired?

The thing that is most painful is the giving up of a skill, of something that you know so well and that you can do and that you understand so fully. I must say that when I realise what I can perceive of a cricket match in five minutes, say, at 50, 100 yards' distance, one of the things that brings out for me is how little I can perceive of other things.

Left: Douglas Jardine (*left*) and Patsy Hendren, Bristol, 1926

Right: Mike Brearley, Middlesex v Lancashire at Lord's, 1976

This is why I don't want to go to cricket matches. I feel I am useless. To go to a cricket match and not be doing anything, makes me feel almost deprived. That series of yours and Botham's, Botham's and yours, against the Australians. I couldn't bear to watch it, I so desperately wanted to be there. And I felt, well, I have got to resolve this now, and at the end of the season, I thought well, I have lived through that, which would have been the greatest of all series to have broadcast and I didn't, so OK, the cords are broken. But they are not completely broken. The commentary has gone but I still retain the presidency of the Cricketers' Association; and I often think of the lady in Oscar Wilde who knew nothing at all about music but was very fond of musicians and I have always got on very well with cricketers.

I think in many ways they are the best community I have ever been in. Local government, mental hospitals, the police, Fleet Street, the stage, BBC, sound radio, television, association football, badminton, fishing, book collecting, antiquarian books, of all the communities I have ever been in, I have found cricket and cricketers the most rewarding. I think in many ways, although there is some slight evidence to the contrary in recent years, on the whole they are the most loyal and generous people, especially since they live in fairly infinite peril really, professional cricketers. There are only 160, 170 of them that are really established and most know at any moment the chopper could fall.

Yes, I know. Each game has that within it, too. It's an extraordinary business. You can get one good ball or you can make one slight mistake and you are out of the game for a day or two days or something. So I think it's built in, the whole idea of loss is built into the game in a very dramatic way.

I always remember dear old Emrys Davies[3] of Glamorgan, who were playing Northampton, I think it was 1954 and Emrys was out in the second innings and he came to Wilf Wooller and he said:

'Skipper, I am going to retire.'

So Wilf said, 'Don't be silly, Em, you will stay for the contract until the end of the season. If you want to renew after that, we want you with us.'

So Em said, 'No, Skipper, you have got to send me home tonight.'

Emrys Davies of Glamorgan

Left: John Arlott in discussion with Trevor Bailey and Denis Compton, 1973

[3] Glamorgan

21

Wilf said, 'You'll come on to the next match.'

But Em said, 'You've got to send me home tonight.'

'Why?'

Em said, 'Look, I have been out more often than you have and I always reckon I know why I was out. I knew why I was out today.'

Wilf said, 'Why was that?'

And Em said, 'This chap Tyson was too fast for me, and I cannot now play his pace so I am going, and I am going tonight, Skipper.'

And you know that seemed to me so tragic, it stopped me in my tracks. That suddenly, in the few seconds it took a fast bowler to bowl, a splendid cricketer – old, wise, skilful – realised that his career was ended. This I think in cricket is even more dramatic than football, probably more dramatic than anywhere else. In football, you see, you can drift out, you can drop out of the first team into the second team, out of the second team into the minor leagues, but cricket is the championship or nothing.

It's such a difficult question. I think people have sometimes toyed with the idea of retiring with me, they have asked me what I think; and on the one hand you feel they have got this fantastic gift and talent and they may never find another area of life – and it may be true for many people, they may never find another area of life that satisfies them in the way that this cricket has satisfied them – and yet on the other hand you don't want people to hang on beyond their welcome. It can end in bitterness and regrets and bad feelings, so it's a very difficult thing.

It's hard, unless you have really got an alternative to your hand, and so few cricketers have, of course, because they have always thought of cricket as the be-all and end-all of things. I can remember – twice this has happened to me – being asked back, giving somebody a lift from a match and they say, 'Come in, come in and have a drink.'

You go in and they produce a scrap-book and you find that for three or four years they hovered on the brink of a county team, and there are the local newspaper cuttings and they played for the second eleven; when they got into the first team they took a good wicket or scored 25 or something like that. You have only got to look at *Wisden* year by year to realise the number of people who come into the edge of County cricket and never make the grade. But it is very easy to forget what infinite happiness it gave them while they were there and now that they may have gone on and become successful businessmen or something like that, still they had the great happiness for those few years of first-class cricket.

Perhaps I romanticise it because I wasn't good enough to play myself.

You have mentioned your father a couple of times. What did he do, what was he like?

He was the cemetery registrar at Basingstoke, forceput. He was a terribly good mechanic, and he was tutored in diesel engines by Doctor Diesel himself, of which he was most proud. It was a shame, he did that you see to get a house for himself and my mother and a secure income before he went to the First World War.

He was quite small, and neat, most capable, superb with his hands; he could do anything in the house, indeed he furnished it in oak. He used to mend our shoes, change the fuses, do the plumbing, do the carpentry, do all the repairs about the house and in addition feed us from the allotment. Of course he worked himself to death. He just worked so hard to keep the family going on a small income, that when he retired there wasn't very much left. But he was such a sweet, gentle, loving, indulgent man. He and my mother were just so wonderful that the poverty never mattered, it never occurred to me. I only stand back and look now and realise how poor we were and am amazed that we were so incredibly happy as a family and how well we understood one another.

There were just the three of you?

Yes, and the doctor, I believe, recommended my mother to have another child and she said, 'Yes, Doctor, I would if only I could afford it,' and it really was like that. But she was a most capable woman. She was the local Liberal agent and did succeed. She was the only one who ever did, the only agent who ever got a Liberal in for Basingstoke.

It sounds as though your relationship with them continued to be really close, there was a lot of communication.

We were always terribly close, yes. I loved them dearly, I was desperately grateful to them, I still am.

It's about the most important thing people do for other people, isn't it?

Yes.

Did your father play sport?

Not at all. The only sport he ever played was bowling under-arm to me when I demanded assistance. No, he wasn't a games player. Magnificent with his hands, not at games.

He made all the furniture?

Yes. All the repairs and the work in the house. He had splendid hands. I am useless, my eldest son was not so hot. The second one, when he went from the junior school to senior school at Highgate, in the valedictory report they said his handicraft was 'cheerfully hopeless'. Robert is different, extremely good with his hands, do anything about the house. I can't wait for him to come home on another holiday to do something else.

So you don't know where it came from, your own interest in sport and ball games?

No, my eldest son, and the second son shared it, mine came almost like a bewildering experience.

My little council school at Basingstoke was opposite the cricket ground, but there was no cricket there all during the First World War. In fact they didn't play any at all until 1921. I was seven, and through the gaps in the oak palings I saw people in white moving inside there, and I went in through the gate, waiting for somebody to bawl me out, and nobody did – they were all too occupied. And I watched this, which seemed to me like magic. My father was away at the war, for long after it ended, they all were, troop ship hold ups and so on, and I went in and watched this . . . I suppose I knew it was cricket. But it was all I did know.

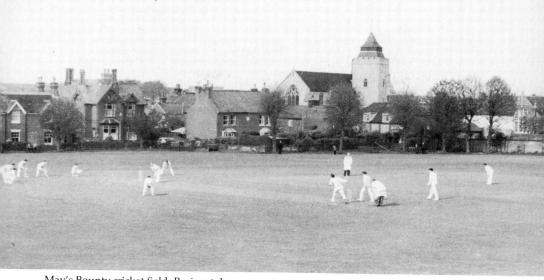

May's Bounty cricket field, Basingstoke

The pavillion at May's Bounty

So you only discovered it from that.

Yes. From that moment I was hooked. Then Hampshire came to play against Basingstoke. They called it Hampshire Club and Ground. At the end of the season, almost a full county side. I remember Lionel Tennyson scoring a hundred and Alec Kennedy bowling Basingstoke out. There they were, the people whose names I had seen in the paper. But what I couldn't understand was the local side, which was Basingstoke and North Hants, were not the people I used to see in the paper as Northants and that baffled me for a very long time.

It baffled me for a moment. It's the ground that's used now and they play championship matches on?

Yes.

Very short straight boundaries. And no doubt the same changing-rooms as they had in the days of . . .

Absolutely the same, we all used them, because old Lieutenant-Colonel John May, who had an MC or TD or something like that, he owned the local brewery and was a man of infinite capacity and generosity. He used to get spectacularly drunk. He bought this cricket ground which was ever after called 'May's Bounty', and left it to the town club and the grammar school. The town club was very proud of it and didn't like the grammar school kicking it up. We used to get pitches right over on the edge, but on the whole they were good to us, very hospitable.

And old Mr Butler went on playing, I don't know, until he was about 150. I don't know, he was ageless, he went on and on and on. He scored his hundreds and he bowled them out and his three sons all played for the town as well. Sometimes he used to permit me to bowl in the nets and actually went so far as to tell me what I was doing wrong, not that it was much help. Oh yes, it was a great help, it made me do it a little less badly than I did before.

Actually the first sum of one pound I ever spent in my life was to become a member of Basingstoke Cricket Club, so that old Bert could help me in the nets. Mind you, he looked a bit dubious when he found out I was a member and could demand the right. He was a great man. A wonderful wise old cricketer, he was; he played once for the county and that was the great imprimatur, when you were a boy in those days. There were no pop stars, no pop heroes, no radio heroes; there was radio, but no radio heroes; and there was no television.

There was a local cinema, and it was owned by a man called Casey who also ran a concert party which performed, I believe, on Ramsgate Pier. Now something used to happen, I think the Ramsgate Pier arrangement ended on the second week of September because the holidaymakers had all gone back, but he had to pay the concert party by the month, so he had got two weeks left. He used to bring them to the Corn Exchange, or the Grand as it was called, at Basingstoke, and somewhere else where he had a theatre. And it was desperately cheap, though more than we could afford, the orchestra stalls were as much as 10d.

The Haymarket Theatre, Basingstoke, before recent extension and alterations

Left: Arlott the hopeful cricketer. Opening the innings for Old St Michael's with Jack Peer, somewhere in Hampshire

And I always remember one boy at school who had been to this, was asked what it was like. It was terrific, he said, the girl at the end of the chorus line, 'her bosom fell out'. And one of the others said, 'Shut up, that was the night before last!' I think that Mr Casey used to increase the attraction of the show by the girl at the end of the chorus line.

Basingstoke Market Place in the 1920s

London Street, Basingstoke, in the 1920s

But you never saw it, never saw Casey's?

Never saw Casey's . . . no. We used to go in at three ha'penny time, that was Saturday afternoons. There was a little bit on the stage then, but it was mainly film.

The Corn Exchange cinema changed to the Grand Theatre. It led out into the lesser market, peanuts for a ha'penny a bag . . . the days of naptha flares in the market . . . a tiny provincial town, now unrecognizable.

Was Basingstoke ever an attractive or a beautiful town? Was it in beautiful countryside?

Lovely countryside all round it, especially the dells. And the town itself had six quite beautiful buildings, all of which, to the best of my knowledge, have been demolished and replaced by the Great Wall of China. It was, I think, the first of the overspill towns. That wise man George Willis the historian of the town, once said, when this London overspill was being discussed, 'Gentlemen, it is no good arguing as to whether this will improve the town or not, because no town has ever been artificially forced to grow before, so we cannot say whether it will be good or not.'

It wasn't the greatest success, I fear. It's got a good sports complex and it's got some rather sad, unhappy housing. People have come down from London where they had friendly neighbours and a little shopping precinct, a yard or two away, into this sprawl of housing, which is the prescription for the slums of the future. Low storey, high density. It's a bit grim. It wasn't a very distinguished town, we did have one or two good houses and everybody knew everybody else. Now nobody knows anybody else.

So you were born in 1914, and you were seven when you first went into the Basingstoke ground and saw this weird thing, and from then on you kept going to all the matches locally and . . .

Yes, playing as much as I could. Seeing Hampshire send terribly strong Club and Ground sides out there and there were really good players in club cricket then, so I saw a lot of them. But I never saw a first-class match until 1926, when I saw the Test Match at the Oval when we recovered the Ashes, which was terrific.

What do you remember of that? Did your father take you?

No. I went by myself, solemnly warned that there were
people at cricket matches who would overcharge boys for
mineral waters. Ate my sandwiches by ten past eleven. Everybody stayed away because they said the crowds would be so
large, they wouldn't get in, yet the ground wasn't even full.

I saw the Hobbs[4]/Sutcliffe[5] partnership and that lovely
innings on the turning wicket against Arthur Richardson but
I didn't really understand what I was looking at, of course. I

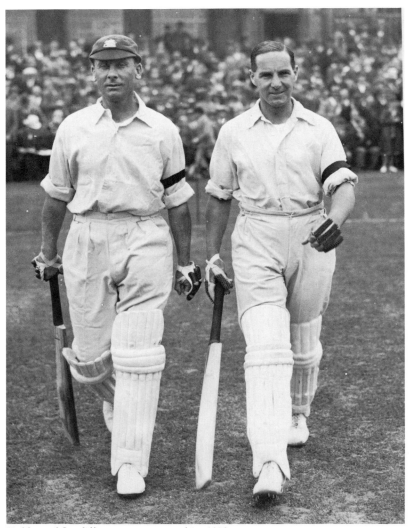

Hobbs and Sutcliffe – a great partnership, 1930

[4] Surrey and England
[5] Yorkshire and England

couldn't see that Jack Hobbs was a good player until I realised that he was pottering about the place, you know, like a man in his garden with a walking stick. Other people were hurrying through their strokes and so on and so forth, but when he was out there smiling at the bowler it all seemed so easy. Not half so spectacular as Len Crate[6] hitting the ball out of May's Bounty, but I gradually came to realise. And I never saw him fail.

But the Test Match was wonderful. You know to have seen the Australians in their baggy caps . . . You see it wasn't easy if you were hard up, it wasn't easy to raise the money to go to London to see a cricket match. It wasn't really easy to go to Southampton.

And then going to Eastbourne and staying with my grandmother and going to see Sussex and watching Tate[7]. I can always remember going, standing by the sight-screen and then lying down and looking under the sight-screen at Eastbourne, and seeing Maurice Tate bowl. He came up and bowled, and then I couldn't see the ball and then suddenly I could see it – it was the outswinger – and then bang – it came back again.

I remember that game. Lancashire were going for the championship. Sussex bowled them out for 91 and 99 and beat 'em by an innings. Sussex made 391 and Charlie Hallows, I think, made 1,000 in May that year or before the end of May. Left-hander. He came in and he was just calmly playing himself in, and Tate bowled him a ball that sort of jumped like that, and he was caught and bowled. He didn't play a stroke. The ball came through and bounced off almost the splice and went back into the bowler's hands before the batsman had realised what had happened.

I'd not realised what swing or pace off the pitch meant until I saw this lovely great rosy smiling man come up and – he'd this great weight of shoulders – when his hand came down it seemed to follow behind the ball and go right through. They used to say he was fast medium through the air and fast off the pitch, and George Cox[8] once told me that often on a wet ground and when Maurice was on song, as that left foot of his came down he, George, felt the ground shake under him at cover point.

Of course, the poor chap smashed his left foot to pieces. In fact, when I knew him in his already later years, he had this boot sole with ribs across it like my fingers to support these smashed bones of the instep. And in 1924/5, you see, he took

---

[6] Basingstoke
[7] Sussex and England
[8] Sussex

Maurice Tate on his way to
the nets and (*below*) bowling
for England, 1932

those 38 wickets and, I don't know, I don't think anybody else took more than 8 against the Australians. They tried to tire him but they couldn't quite do it. It was Adelaide I think when he bowled through with a boot full of blood.

He was a prodigious man, with his big feet and bigger heart, somebody once said. Tom Webster drew him so beautifully. I knew him quite well in his late years and had the luck to clear up his estate and, oh, they were a wonderful family, the Tates, and he the greatest of them. The best and biggest of hearts. You'd see those two in the same match and they would become *my* bowler and *my* batsman . . .

What, Tate and Hobbs? Mm. And who was he like as a bowler, who followed him, Maurice Tate, is there anyone?

I suppose most of all like Alec Bedser.[9] A great difference was that Alec was basically an inswinger. Maurice was basically an outswinger. Harold Gilligan, who captained him for a long time, used to say Maurice would never say, 'I'm tired, I want to come off.' But when he asked for an extra short leg, Harold knew he was getting tired because he was bowling inswingers. And he had this immense pace off the pitch that Alec Bedser didn't quite have, in fact nobody else has ever had.

Bob Wyatt,[10] who is, I suppose, the most observant of cricket players with the best analytical brain for technique that I have known, says there never was anybody like Maurice. As Bob said, if he didn't gain pace off the pitch he lost less than anybody else.

I was struck by reading in your writing about him that he bowled one wide in his life and no no-balls. That's remarkable.

No no-balls. You see he was a slow bowler in his early days, he'd bowl slow, slow medium off-spinners like his father. And one day he got so fed up with old Philip Mead, who was plodding along towards a century at Horsham – well, as he put it to me, 'I let him have one.'

I said, 'And what happened, Maurice?'

He said, 'Very funny, very funny. Dipped into him and went away and hit the top of the off stump.' He said, 'I didn't know what to say,' which is typical Maurice, that.

I saw Philip a few weeks later and I recited this to him and said, 'Is that true?'

'Yes,' he said. 'Young cub – didn't even know he could bowl

[9] Surrey and England
[10] Warwickshire, Worcestershire and England

Philip Mead

a quick one. Wonderful ball pitched leg hit off.'
   So I said, 'Did you say anything to him, Philip?'
   'Oh, no,' he said, 'I never encouraged bowlers.'
   And I'm sure he didn't.

Old Philip Mead, you know, was a wonderful man who
wouldn't take a net. Alec Kennedy used to pull his leg and
he'd say, 'You lead in May, I shall catch you in June.' And one
year he had a bad May – I'm not very good about the actual
figures – when people were saying, 'You're a bit short on the
old talent money, Philip,' and he proceeded to go into the
month of June and make 1,360 runs in eleven innings, two of
them not out. And there was that famous game they had to

follow on, not the historic revival one against Warwickshire, but in those days, you know, they didn't really go for a third day finish. Hampshire batted: all out for a hundred. They had to follow on, and he just picked up his bat again and went out and made a hundred. Everybody tells me it's not true that a Gurkha won't unsheath his kukri or he won't sheath it again without drawing blood. But old Philip wasn't in the least bit interested in batting, only in making runs, because he made more runs for Hampshire than any other man in the history of the game for any team at all. 48,000's an awful lot, isn't it?

Well, I happened to see about two minutes of Phil Mead on film, and, oh, he must have been about fifty at the time, and wherever they bowled it all he did was work everything round to square leg and long leg. He can't always have played like that, can he?

Wilfred Rhodes

No. He could play all the strokes, but he did have this weakness for the leg side.

After he was blind, he used to come along to the cricket at Bournemouth, and sit in the players' dressing-room, and he was always very welcome. And he would listen to the cricket, you know, and sometimes when he was sitting with old Wilfred Rhodes[11] they'd ask him in as well, and there were the two blind men listening to the cricket. And once I was sitting by Philip and he said, 'You know, that young Rogers, he's edging them.' I said, 'Yes, I don't think he wants to play the full stroke there against Cliff Gladwin.'[12] He said, 'Why, what do you mean?' I said, 'Well, he's bowling inswingers.' 'Lovely stuff,' he said, 'lovely stuff. Where are his fieldsmen?' So I told him where Cliff's legtrap was, you see, and he said, 'Worse than Fred Root.[13] He'd have cost me twelve an hour in leg glances, wouldn't he?' He was another of the sound men who never said they were better in his time than later.

Alec Bedser, 1950

[11] Sussex and England
[12] Derbyshire
[13] Worcestershire and England

Not only were you a cemetery keeper's son, but you failed your School Certificate.

Spectacularly, yes.

Spectacular, was it?

Well, I mean, one subject I would have passed in, might have got a credit in, which was geography. I left halfway through the paper, knowing I had done enough to pass. I went to see Reading play in a cup-tie, and for that reason they turned me down and failed me, which I always thought was a dirty trick. But I took it after I had left school. I left school in rebellion.

Why was that? What happened at school? What was your school?

It was Queen Mary's School, Basingstoke, which was a little grammar school of 125 boys, tough and hard, with a Prussian headmaster who enjoyed wielding the cane. We looked each other in the eye very early on, and I think he thought he could beat me into submission. I had more whacks than anybody else in our form. 'Touch your toes,' and he whipped your coat tails up and back, and out of his gown he pulled this cane which was as thick as my thumb and four feet long. He always used to cane up against the wash basins because there it echoed all round the school. The bruises lasted for about a fortnight, red the first night and gradually getting black. You would take a three or a four and stand up and look him in the eyes. I never had a six, I never did anything quite bad enough to deserve that, but I never saw anybody keep consciousness after he had one of Percival's sixes. They would fall on their face or stagger out and people in the form would catch them and take them out and run their head under the tap at the basins. But he enjoyed it, poor fellow, and he had asthma so you can feel sorry for him.

Queen Mary's School, Worting Road, Basingstoke

But it set you against the whole school process?

Well, I had friends there and there were some staff that I respected immensely, but it set me against him so that I had to get level even, though I couldn't afford it, to the extent of smoking the same expensive cigarettes.

I did put it straight years afterwards when, bewilderingly, he turned up at an Old Boys' dinner and they asked me to propose his health. I said, 'Me? You know what I thought of him,' and the chairman said, 'Yes, say it,' and I said it, and still don't know whether it was cruel or deserved or valedictory, or whether he had asked for it and deserved to know before he died. But if he is listening now I meant it. That I think taught me the great lesson, that violence gets you nowhere, brutality gets you nowhere.

John, the food that you have often given me in your house, and the meals I have enjoyed so much, they have always been very traditional meals, meat and vegetables and cheese and wine, and not much in the way of sweets and fancy things like that. Has that always been?

No, I used to be very fond of sweets, but if you have got my girth you have to watch it.

I used to eat vast quantities of cheese with immense enthusiasm, it's the one thing I think I have never tired of in my entire life. Funnily enough my youngest son will come down and cut himself cheese for breakfast.

But I am sure it's right to have cheese and wine together, I am sure the cheese and wine party is a good idea. I don't know if it's ever occurred to you, cheese and wine are man's two most successful attempts to turn the temporary into the permanent. He has preserved his milk in cheese which sometimes will keep for years and his grapes in wine, which will keep perhaps for centuries.

I have never been a slavish food eater, and at the same time I have never been a slavish wine drinker. I think the two belong together.

What do you mean by slavish?

I have never sat around drinking just for drinking's sake, at least perhaps not since I swilled beer in my late teens. But I do care for the traditional, not only traditional English but traditional French, and that surely goes really with people and with sitting round the table and talking, as the French do far more than the English, who will take a television meal on their laps, with a tray, of course. I must say if you need more entertainment than food, wine, your friends and their conversation you had better have a television, but I have never found it a necessity.

Above and **Right**: John Arlott photographed in the cellar of his house in Alresford, Hampshire

Funny, you see I have worked in radio and television and I have never known really very much about either. I remember when I was a little boy and my father made our first crystal set, listening to a banjo on earphones. But then you see I used to go out in the evenings, playing cricket, playing football, playing bridge in my bridge-playing phase. Then courting, then leaving home and going into digs where they didn't want you in their room listening to their radio. Then I married and had my own, but then came the war, so you didn't much look in or listen in. After the war, a question of working, going to London and being all eyes and ears for London and then this influence of the French, so I have never really much listened to radio or looked at television except the 'Today' programme in the mornings. That is the ideal bathroom companion; you can shave, shampoo, think or anything you like, stand on your head, while that is on. I find it infinitely entertaining. But that and the 5.40 news and that's it. For the rest, work through the day, and dine through the evening.

How did you get interested in wine and food? I presume that your mother was a jolly good cook, that was the start?

Yes, and I always had a good appetite. Up to '48, '49, I used to drink a lot of whisky and it didn't do me any good. I came back from South Africa on that wonderful old speedbird trip, seven

40

days on a flying boat. It put down on the Nile and so on and so forth. The last stop was Augusta, Sicily, and I looked at myself in the mirror and I thought, if I go home looking like this people are going to think I drank in South Africa as much as I have drunk.

So I rang up the girl in the office and said, 'Is it all right for me to break my journey here?' She said, 'Not for more than six months, sir,' and I said, 'No, not for more than six months, I would just like to stay over for a week. Where could I stay?'

She said, 'You could stay in the airline hotel here in Augusta where you are now, where no doubt you would get a favourable rate, but at this time of the year Taormina is the loveliest place in the world with all the spring flowers in bloom.' So I went up there and went into a little hotel, pensione, and solemnly for three days I did not drink, although there was a carafe of wine on the table as there might be a carafe of water in an English boarding-house. I reminded myself of the old saws about the wine of the country and I put out my hand and poured and from that moment on I was hooked. I have never drunk beer or spirits since, except occasional medicinal brandy.

The next day I went down the hill and I met two Americans who were taking their demobilisation pay and a holiday travelling round Europe. We started to talk and they said, 'Have you drunk this wine?' I agreed that I had and we talked about it and I said that the landlord of my little boarding-house was the brother of a vigneron up the mountain, wine grower, and they ought to come up and taste his wine. So all of us went back up the hill and the landlord brought out his best bottles for us, when he heard he had been boasted about.

The next day he took us up the mountain to meet his brother who told us that we ought to go to Syracuse and the wines we should try there and where we could go and try them. We said we didn't know how to get there and he knew somebody who was going into Syracuse the next day on behalf of most of the village and was coming back with all the shopping. So he sent us down and we had, I think, the most strikingly educational day of my life. I learnt more about wine that day than in all the rest of my life and I got home so hooked that I hurried off buying wine books.

I dashed off to France, and had the luck to go on an identical tour of Bordeaux and the claret country, first of all with a press party and then a month later the BBC were coming out, to do a feature on claret with André Simon and Laurence Gilliam and Wynford Vaughan-Thomas, and they said I could stay on and go round with them. So I stayed a month in Daniel Querre's Château Monbousquet, where they taught me how to drink, at least how to drink claret, and how to eat. I came back, and then I made the second tour. You must have encountered this. If you learn something once and there is a pause, while subconsciously you digest it and then you get the same lesson over again, and you will learn five times as much the second time as you did the first.

Wynford Vaughan-Thomas on an outside broadcast, August 1949

Laurence Gilliam, September 1962

I came back and changed my entire lifestyle, even the look of the dining-table, what was on it and how we ate and drank. And I learnt there, coincidentally, to go without television because, as you know, at this table we sit and eat and drink and take our coffee and talk until we go to bed, entertaining ourselves. That's what taught me that, Italy first, France second.

Then when I came to this house, I found that over the top of the door were carvings of vine leaves and grapes in the stonework. We knew that Fred Odoire had grapes here at the start of the century, but never realised that in the first place when it was built they were going to plant or grow vines here, and that's 110 years ago. So I was able to change the name of the house from Balmoral, which used to make my friends split their sides, to The Vines by planting vines of my own, which with any luck we will one day get some wine from.

You told me once that you lived a lot of your life being afraid that you wouldn't have enough wine for your retirement, and then you ended up thinking you wouldn't be able to drink it.

Yes, it is a very difficult situation and when I came to move over here I had to decide not only whether I could move six and a half thousand bottles of wine over to Alderney, but also, which I resented, pay the Guernsey duty, having already paid mainland duty on it. I decided I couldn't and Christie's took it and said it was the most catholic collection of wine, the most wide-ranging collection of wine, they had ever sold. I must say when I saw the list I could only agree; I had some strange stuff.

For many years, John Arlott's wine column has appeared in *The Guardian*

WINE

John Arlott

He is photographed here in a Beaujolais cellar

But there are great wines that people hardly recognise: Colares, the quite great Portuguese wine that nobody ever bothers to talk about; Tokay Essencia, some of the fine Italians, Vino Nobile di Montepulciano, Brunello di Montal-cino, recent wines too. There are great wines in almost every wine-producing country, Germany in particular. I don't drink a great deal of German wine, but some of them no doubt are quite splendid. Some of them age 200, 300 years before they die.

And a collection of wine is a wonderful thing. You get mean about it, of course, and you think, 'My wife is not going to have this Château Latour 1934 to put in the onion soup or Irish stew.' But sometimes you just like somebody who you know enjoys it, and you go downstairs and you rub the dust off and you bring it up and give it to them and then the expression on their faces is such a reward. To taste a great wine really does things to a wine drinker. I think it is one of the great pleasures. Who was it said the greatest pleasure in the world is 'to have known the best and to have known it for the best'? Because the second is the essential qualification – if you have not only tasted a great wine, but you have known it's a great wine.

The other side of you in that respect has also been that you can say that wine is only the juice of a grape and it is there to be enjoyed because it tastes good.

Ah yes, that is true, but there's good and good and good; there are degrees of good until you reach great.

You kept a bit of the collection?

Well, I didn't keep any in the first place, but I kept going up to Christie's and clawing it back because I felt I couldn't bear to part with it and anyway I have built a new collection here. It's a rather smaller cellar, but there are so few cellars in Alderney anyway I was lucky to get one. It still has the trip-wire that the Germans fixed, not linked to an explosive charge any longer, but the trip wire is still there.

John Betjeman was a good friend of yours, wasn't he?

Oh, he was. He was an immense influence on me. I think I would never have tried to write poetry if it hadn't been for him. The first anthology I ever made with George Rostrevor Hamilton was based on the Betjeman topographical poetic theme, and he was my middle son's godfather. Always a funny man, with an immense streak of sincerity and depth of feeling and as independent a thinker I suppose as there has been in this century in Britain.

And you shared quite a few of his views, didn't you? A lot of your poetry was about English towns and places and crafts?

Indeed, as I say, he had an immense influence on me in that respect. I only wish I had been as good as he is.

John Betjeman, 1955

I imagine that he also actually influenced what you did do creatively, which was, among other things, broadcast on cricket?

Yes, you see the good poet in his imagery defines. He describes precisely. He doesn't say, 'That was a good stroke,' 'This is a pretty cricket ground,' 'This is a good-looking man.' He says what it is: 'This is a poised, graceful, well-timed, powerful, or whatever, stroke.' 'This is an old-fashioned looking ground, a leafy-tree-ground with an Edwardian pavilion, or a Victorian pavilion, or a modern pavilion.' I think if you are trying to describe things to people that is the sort of thing you have got to say in a commentary, say what you see. You see, it's easy to be a commentator, I am sure, to bring out statistics, and a terrific number of people are vastly interested in statistics – 'he now wants so many runs to do so and so' – and I always had Bill Frindall to tell me that, but for me it was in through the eyes and out through the mouth.

Something happened in between.

There was a digestion process, yes, because there was an editing process, but you say what you see, although every man sees something different. In fact in my younger days I have been known to observe attractive young women walking round the ground and that type of thing.

You mean in your younger days only, of course!
This is a big topic, but I read that somebody said of you, in your early days at the BBC, that you had a superior mind and a vulgar voice.

That's right.

I wondered if people tried to change you from being what you were.

Well, I tried to change my voice once. One Thursday, I was producing a programme and Val Dyall came in, Valentine Dyall, and after a bit he said, 'John. Are you trying to do something to your voice?' 'Well,' I said, 'I am trying not to sound too much like a country bumpkin. I'd like to get on to as they say standard southern English.' 'You fool,' he commented. 'Everybody in this studio can speak that; you are the only one that can speak authentic Hampshire. Don't, for God's sake, throw that away.'

John Arlott developing the art of commentary, August 1949

And I thought, well, I suppose he is right and it was going to be a bit of an effort.

But you do it anyway, you know. I went back home once, I remember, after I had been to the police training school, the Birmingham police training school, for the Southampton force. I had been back about a month, and I had been away for a couple of months, and my mother said, 'You had better go out and see the men,' – the men who were grass cutting outside – so I went over and said hello, how were they. They quizzed me about Southampton: was it true there were trains and trams running through the streets – these were very old men – and I said, yes it was. And it went on and on, and after a bit one of them looked at me and said, 'And what be this here London talk you are putting on then, eh?' I never thought that fifty years ago mine was 'London talk'!

Valentine Dyall, 1976

But the first recording I ever made, I did a Light Programme first. Then I was asked to come on 'Country Magazine' and we knew there was a repeat going out at half past five in the morning on Overseas. It takes a lot to get me out of bed at that time, but we got up and switched this programme on and I can imagine how my face fell. I said, 'Dear oh dear,' and my wife said, 'What's the matter?' I said, 'That's the script I did, but they've got this country chap reading it.' So she threw back her head and laughed, 'That's you, you fool!' I had never heard my recorded voice, I never dreamt it was like that.

I think it's a shock for everyone, isn't it, the first time you hear it?

It seemed to me that I was ruined for ever. I was never going to get this career in broadcasting I had come to dream about.

But with a bit of good advice and with your own personality you stuck with it and you cut your own path, didn't you? It was a new thing, what you were doing, wasn't it? Certainly in sport?

It was in a way, yes. We used to play back the discs and Howard Marshall had done it, but a bit behind the play. There had never been I think, previously, much attempt at precise visual description. After I went on the instructional staff, I used to get every record I could and play them back, but I couldn't find anybody that had had any immense visual urge. It's just your own particular bent, I suppose. You expose your own mind and you never do it more than in commentary

Rain stops play at Scarborough, 1946. Commentator John Arlott and friendly BBC engineer see the shower through

when you are speaking absolutely ad lib and you don't know what is going to happen in the next second. It's got to come out and the funny thing was, I used to find that if I was writing about a day's play, I tended not to remember the play that I had done the commentary on because that went in and out. Funny, you retained other things. But you had to cast your mind back and make a deliberate effort to pick up what you had done the commentary on; it was almost as if you had purged yourself.

It's about as immediate as you can get, isn't it?

Yes, I always used to think that if you could get the man caught at the wicket before the crowd shouted you were up with the ball.

Yes, one of the things I find myself doing sometimes, when there is a photograph in a cricket book of a dismissal, is looking at the beginnings of recognition in the crowd. They are just starting and the stump's on the ground by then or the man's already started to walk.

Yes, it's funny. There is nothing in cricket, to my mind – not even a spectacular six – there is nothing so exciting as the fall of a wicket.

I agree.

And when a side is running through another's batting and wickets are going down quickly, you hear this sound, almost like the baying of a pack of hounds, every time a wicket falls. They are hounding the side that is being bowled out. I often think that sides are bowled out for small totals, almost psychologically, after the first three or four wickets are down, it's as if they can feel the ground waiting to roar again. It used to be like this at the Oval when Bedser, Loader, Surridge, Lock, Laker, with Eric Bedser in reserve, were bowling out sides and when they first started to win the championship before the crowds dwindled. People used to go, almost like the crowd at a gladiatorial contest, to watch the other side torn to pieces.

That reminds me of the famous '74/5 series in Australia, when Lilley and Thompson demolished us on some bad wickets. Towards the end of the series, the England players used to refer to the seat reserved for

Denis Lillee in rampant form against England's Mike Gatting
Third Test, England v Australia, July 1981, at Leeds

the next batsman in as the condemned cell, and I think this wasn't just
healthy 'hangdog' humour. They got the message very well.

Yes, there is no doubt that communicates to a crowd more
than anything else, the destruction of the opponents. Hitting
a six, all right, spectacular, beautiful, like that glorious stroke
on to the roof of Lord's pavilion by Kim Hughes, but there is
nothing quite to compare with bowling right through a side.

Going back to the early days of your cricket watching, you weren't in Australia when body-line was used, were you?

No, but I saw it happen. I saw it invented. I saw it first started and I know my facts are right because I talked it over with Douglas Jardine,[14] fifteen years afterwards.

My schoolfriend John Carter and I used to take a fortnight's holiday and we'd go to stay in London. We would go to cricket by day and theatre by night, which coming up from the country was a great thing to do. And one day we decided we'd go and see the third day's play between Essex and Notts. Notts were doing well in the championship, and we went over to Leyton. That's when I learned how big London was. We got in a bus at Cambridge Circus and it took, it seemed, half a day to get to Leyton. You know, grey ammunition boxes to sit on.

Anyway, Notts were batting along nicely, and it got to lunch and they declared with Willis Walker 99 not out, which I shall never forget since I've never seen that happen before or since. Arthur Carr I'm sure had told him, 'I'll declare at lunch whatever happens.'

Well, Voce and Larwood bowled four overs, two apiece. And then Larwood went back to bowl the fifth. And John and I looked at each other and he said,

'Look at the field.'

'Voce can't bowl two consecutive overs,' I said.

'No, he's not going to.'

'Then,' I said, 'Larwood's going to bowl off-breaks.'

'Not with the wicket-keeper there, he isn't,' he replied.

'He's going to bowl at his head.'

'Yes,' he said.

So, he bowled this short stuff and so did Bill Voce to a packed leg-side field. They didn't do it very well actually – Maurice Nicholls I think got a hundred – they only took two

[14] Surrey and England

Douglas Jardine

Arthur Carr

1932 -3 *Tests*
33 WKTS average 19·51

Larwood and Voce

wickets and they didn't win. We came away, two 18-year-olds, utterly baffled. We couldn't understand this. You know, we had reached the sort of know-all stage about cricket. This wouldn't do in Australia. Australians had great hookers; bowl short and they'd hook you out of sight.

Anyway we couldn't see them again until, I think, it was about the last match of the season, when they were going to play Glamorgan at Cardiff. And we got on our bikes to Reading and caught the milk train to Cardiff and went down that night. And sure enough they bowled it again and Maurice Turnbull, who was one of the greatest of all hookers, hooked 'em out of sight, got a century, and we came back so baffled we didn't even mention it to anybody.

But when body-line started in Australia, that's what we saw. We saw the start of it. And I asked Douglas Jardine about this and he said yes, they'd decided that Bradman's weakness was a short ball on or outside his legs. The people who could deliver it were Larwood and Voce. He discussed it with Arthur Carr and Arthur said all right, they would bowl it that season whenever it was practicable.

He'd talked about it before they even went to Australia, Jardine?

Yes.

I didn't realise that.

Arthur Carr put them on, to do it for him.

I've heard Harold Larwood talk about it, talking about how if the ball was swinging he bowled with three or four slips and a gulley. But he said that in Australia it didn't swing for long, and after six or seven overs all the slips would go over the other side. It was a pretty awful thing, though, wasn't it? No restriction on the field, no restriction of behind-square fielders.

Yes it was, but, you see, again it was almost historic inevitability. The Australians used fast bowling against us in 1921 and again in 1948 and, immediately after the war, we had no domestic fast bowling and our batsmen were out of practice against it. You see in 1954/5 when Tyson and Statham[15] bowled them out, they had no fast bowling in their domestic cricket.

Left: Brian Statham

Right: his partner, Frank Tyson, in action for England

[15] Lancashire and England

The real strength had been Miller and Lindwall and they were no longer as fast as they had been, while we had a fleet of fast bowlers and we had Tyson bowling at that bit of extra pace. And the same happened in '32/3. They had no real fast bowlers, otherwise they would have hooked Larwood and Voce more savagely than they did. Though it is difficult to see how, if people as fast as that were pounding away like that.

It's difficult also for me to imagine having enough control over it, to be able to hook safely when you've no limit on the fielders behind square. I think it's one of the best changes in the laws that was brought in – to restrict the fieldsmen behind square. The only drawback is that the off-spinner can't attack on a turning wicket in the way that he might, because he often has to have somebody back for the sweep. He can't have two short legs behind him.

Yes, you can't distinguish between the fast bowler and the slow bowler for the purpose of legislation.

That's right. But you took it up as well, didn't you, John? I mean following on from Larwood and Voce, it was Larwood, Voce and Arlott, wasn't it?

Yes, in a match at Tylney Hall, I would have ruined my aunt's love life by bowling bouncers at her boyfriend, she said.

6 for 21?

28.

6 for 28.

Mm, best analysis of my life. They cancelled the fixture. We went in and this little chap bowling off-breaks that didn't bowled us out for 51, and every year he used to do me playing for the turn. We got 51, and Jack Peer[16] said, 'Well, that's it.'
    I said, 'No. We'll get 'em out, bowling the same stuff England bowled in Australia.'
    'Who's going to bowl it?' he asked. 'You, I suppose.'
    I said, 'Yes.'
    'You can have two overs,' he said.
    I had her boyfriend caught at slip, defending his face at the fifth ball of the first over. That's my solitary worthwhile fast-bowling escapade and, as I said, they cancelled the fixture as a result.

And he threw over your aunt?

Mm, he left my aunt and never spoke to her again.

Perhaps she was well out of it.

Possibly. She didn't exactly favour me for a bit afterwards.

[16] Captain of Old St. Michael's

John, football was quite a big part of your life, wasn't it? Playing and then writing on it?

Yes, it was. I remember in 1921 my mother and father taking me to see Basingstoke win the Hampshire League. Perhaps it wasn't 1921, perhaps it was the Hampshire Cup, whatever it was, it was terribly important. And then I took to going to Reading, completely dedicated. I used to cycle 16 miles each way to see them play, usually evening matches because I loved to be playing myself on Saturday afternoons.

I can still remember that side that went up from the third division to the second in the twenties: Duckworth, Inglis – no – Duckworth, Eggo, McConnell, Inglis, Messer, Evans, Wilson, Braithwaite, Davey, Richardson, Robson.

It was a long time ago, but I remember everybody. A very excitable Duckworth in goal, bald-headed Bert Eggo who played himself into the limbo when Stoke City scored six against them one Easter. Billy McConnell, big, fair haired Irishman, was really a Corinthian type of player who used to run across in front of forwards and whip the ball off their toes; Inglis the hard square-built man; Alf Messer, dominant centre-half; little Dai Evans, the Welsh international, who made a sad exit with Huddersfield when life became too much for him one day; Wilson, a very professional little outside-right; Braithwaite with the long jaw, great dribbler and Davey the Irish international; Frank Richardson; a fiery little inside-left from Swindon; Robson the big outside left – they are all still real to me as they were then.

For years I followed Reading and still I look for their score, although I look second for them now. I look for Southampton first, Reading second. But I would have hated it if they had in the event gone under. Once, of course, they reached the FA Cup semi-final. Oh, it was all very exciting; they were heroes, they were more than lifesize.

After that I reported football professionally and enjoyed it immensely until it just became too seedy. I had two punch-ups in railway trains, nasty punch-ups. I was slugged with a knuckle duster in one of them, which raised the most spectacular bruise on my forehead.

What, you mean just picked on?

Well this looked like being a bad one. But I was in a first class carriage and I fortunately had a wine bottle with me – so I said 'the first man who comes get this.' So they pulled the glass down and spat over me. This was the Manchester United fan club and they were getting out at Leamington – they were the locals – the team had been playing the semi-final in Birmingham – and one of them came by this door with the window dropped and he said 'I never wanted any trouble, I'm sorry,' and I dropped my hands and said 'neither did I,' and he hit me with this knuckleduster over my eye. So as he turned round I hit him in the back of the neck and he skidded across the railway platform. And the guard I think realised something odd was on, so I thought I'd better stay in the carriage.

Then I had another nasty fight on the train down to Winchester. Then I was invited to go and do a match on Boxing Day at Luton and I thought, what a nasty obit to have, 'He was clubbed to death outside the Luton ground.' Now if it had been 'Spurs ground or Arsenal's ground, all right, but there are some places you wouldn't wish to be clubbed to death outside and I suddenly decided I was never going to report any football again. Then I did, so that David Lacey and Frank Keating could go on a *Guardian* tour to India. I finished out that season, but I have never been to a football match since. I was finally sickened.

You know, the dirt isn't all at the bottom end; there is a lot of dirt practised by the players and a lot of financial blackmail, but also at higher levels. Alf Ramsey, for example, took England to win the World Cup and but for a single goalkeeping error he might have done it a second time, but they decided to sack him. Admittedly they had available that intelligent, sensitive, successful, noble and loyal man Don Revie, whom they appointed at twice Ramsey's salary, and you know the wonderful thing that Alf said about his dismissal was when they gave him a farewell banquet. I don't think they asked him to pay for it, either, which is surprising. Alf made his farewell speech, and he stood up and said, 'My

Sir Alf Ramsey, manager of the England side which won the World Cup in 1966 and
narrowly failed to repeat the feat in 1970

lords, ladies and gentlemen, this is an occasion I shall never remember'; either that, or 'This is an occasion I shall always forget.' Whichever it was, by gum he was right. When they could do that to a man as good as that, then that for my money made the whole lot of them a bit seedy. It made them seem to me the sort of chaps who would do anything for eight million pounds in preference to four.

There are nice chaps in it, of course there are, blokes like Joe Mercer and Lawrie McMenemy and Billy Nick, and so on, a lot of them, but still outnumbered two thousand to one. I wouldn't want anything to do with it any more. Sometimes you see the danger of cricket being tainted with the same thing, but usually only the roughs and the drunks, not at the higher levels.

You have never had the highest opinions of the administrators of football have you?

No, I haven't. They are often successful businessmen who usually know nothing at all about football and sack managers who do, because they don't yet understand that only one team can be at the top of any particular league. Third-rate people often, and I wouldn't want to know them any more.

What about the players of football whom you have loved watching, and the skills and the genius of it?

I think the greatest condemnation of them is this new legislation for the professional foul. It has become a cynical game, and it used to be so much a game of self-expression. A dribbler like Westwood or somebody enjoyed himself and you felt the enjoyment as he ran, though he probably lost it in the end. Braithwaite at Reading, Curtis, they were beautiful ball players, but then the cynical foul killed them. I remember Jimmy McIlroy saying to Maurice Edelston[17] once, 'The difference, Maurice, between your day and now, is that in your day if you beat a man you went clear, now if you beat a man you know he is going to bring you down from behind.' And that is the difference, that is the cynical difference, because winning means so much and you see the managers control it. Players don't play as they want to play, they play as their managers tell them to play. No doubt this makes for great efficiency and the managers are paid vast sums for teaching people to do what they want them to do and not what the men themselves

[17] Reading footballer and much-capped England international

want to do, but I think this has fundamentally poisoned the game, that and the supporters.

Good football, I always used to think, was warfare without bloodshed. Now it's warfare with accompanying bloodshed all too often. It's a shame, because it could be a game that gives immense pleasure. People like Corinthian Casuals, who we used to think were a bit up-market, have managed to maintain their standards and their criteria, but not many have. What was the old description? Somebody asked the difference between soccer and rugby and someone else said, 'Well, one is a game for gentlemen played by hooligans and the other's a game for hooligans played by gentlemen.' It's hard to make that distinction nowadays.

Rugby is not so gentlemanly either.

No.

When we discuss dramatic moments, I'm reminded of another of your interests, totally different and miles away, but you've enjoyed bullfighting, haven't you?

Yes, I have. I can shudder at what happens to the horses, but I once saw Pepe Dominguin execute a veronica and send the bull behind him and the horns went through the skin-tight silk pantaloon and the pantaloon fell down and showed his bare back. He never flinched half an inch, with that great bull's horn going through there, which could have smashed him to pieces. The bravery of the good bullfighter and the skill of the good bullfighter; it's almost as if he partners the bull in a dance so that if he makes a false step he's dead. It is savage, of course

The drama of the bullfight

it's savage, but there's an immense beauty and an immense, infinite skill about it.

I couldn't bear it every day. But I've been four consecutive days in the fiesta and never been bored.

This identity of the opponents and the closeness of the rivals – I think that's very central to the heart of cricket, to come back to cricket.

Yes, it is.

The individual – I mean it's a team game, but, as you've said, it's a team game which is the closest thing to an individual contest that there is.

That's true. Nobody in the world is so lonely as the opening batsman taking the first ball from a fast bowler. Unless it's the fast bowler who feels the ball may slip and he may bowl a wide or something. But really, the loneliness of the opening batsman: the loneliness of the long-distance runner doesn't come near for intensity.

And the closeness with your opponent. He's only just down there and the skills can be admired. It's the mutual admiration of bowler and batsman in this contest.

That's right. The age-long conflict of the bowler to overcome the batsman. All the new tactics – but you see incredibly, if you could watch a Hambledon match you'd recognise it; the different gear, the underarm bowling, the two-stump wicket, the curved bat, the different types of stroke, the different field placings; and yet even now after all those years of change, the changes have been so true to character that it's exactly the same game.

John, you have written at least one hymn, and that wasn't all that long ago, was it?

It *was* a long time ago, in fact, late forties, I suppose. I wrote three or four hymns for the BBC hymnbook, one of which is pretty constantly reprinted, more reprinted than anything else I've ever written, I think. A Harvest Festival hymn. Yes, anything to turn an honest penny.

Presumably there was some belief behind it?

Yes, I was brought up to go to church and I was brought up a practising Christian. The loss of my eldest son hit that pretty hard. All very well for people to tell me about that being all for the best and things, but it hasn't changed much with the years, except that other things have joined it. I rate my family higher than anything else in the world, and too many of them have gone. You see, you either belong to the club of it happens to me, or the club of it doesn't happen to me, and never the twain shall meet. That's a corny thing to say, but it is true. We really don't understand each other and can't win them all. Luck over some things and not over others. That's pretty corny and trite too. And I needn't have said it, maybe I shouldn't have said it. Anyway, talk about something else.

I tell you one thing I would like to ask you about, remotely in connection with your family, and that is, did they get enough of you? I mean, did you have enough time? You have been so busy it seems to me.

This is just. I think my absence broke up my first marriage. I was on overseas tours, away on programmes, commentaries, travelling up and down the country, which my marriage couldn't stand. In the second one all that was understood, and so far as I can ever ascertain there were no flaws. Sometimes Robert says, when he comes over here, that I ought not to be working, but I don't work all the time, certainly not if he is here. I think he accepts that.

One of the aspects of that was being a professional, wasn't it, and doing the jobs properly, not turning things down?

Yes, I think I am not so reluctant now, but you see for a long time as a freelance you think, 'If I refuse this job I may never get another.' And especially when I left the BBC and the shelter of a permanent, pensionable job and set out into the wilderness that my father so dreaded, there was then a time when I accepted anything, right, left and centre. If it was work I took it. For years of course I never took a holiday. But Maurice Edelston cured that. He turned up one day and said,
  'When are you two going on holiday, then?' Valerie looked the other way.
  'I don't think we are,' I answered.
  'Why not take the girl for a holiday?' he demanded.
  'But, Maurice, there is so much work to do and if you are a freelance . . .'
  'I am a freelance,' he said, 'and I am going on holiday. Why don't you make him take you somewhere?' And Valerie said,
  'You did say you would take me to Venice.'
  'OK, we will go to Venice,' I said, 'and what's more we will go on the Orient Express.'
  So I rapidly accepted a job, to write an account of a Test tour and dashed it down every night so that as soon as the cricket season ended, we could dive off and get on this train at Victoria.
  Oh dear, oh dear, this was the romantic dream of all times, this was the Orient Express. They took the diner off at Paris on the way out; we went on the way out in a cabin where there wasn't room for two people to stand up at the same time, or even one to stand upright. On the way out, we were next door to the toilet which reeked to high heaven of ammonia. On the way back we were at the opposite end, half a mile walk to the toilet, and I am not sure which was worse. On the way back, also, they took the diner off at Milano.

Arlott, the raw BBC producer, 1946

But the exciting thing was that to eat you bought off those trolleys on the railway platforms. In Switzerland you could get off and you had forty minutes for a meal on the border, in a railway buffet. A railway buffet in this country means everything a railway buffet means in this country, but there it doesn't. So often, you know, you go to a French town and the best restaurant in the town is the railway buffet, and this was like that or it tasted like it in Switzerland.

We had the most magnificent time in Venice. I don't know which is the finest city in the world, whether it's London, Paris, Vienna, Venice or Rome. Bordeaux is close in the running, and Beaune, the walled, boozy city of Burgundy, or Beaujeu, the little, forgotten town of Beaujolais. I don't know. Barcelona? I rather liked San Francisco, but on the whole there are not many of my sort of cities outside Europe, I would think.

Sydney takes a bit of beating.

Trouble is it's full of Australians.

There are exceptions.

There are exceptions. There are some very nice Australians and Sydney is in many ways, I suppose, the most attractive of really modern cities. If you can put up with the taxi drivers.

The first time I ever hailed a cab, he pulled up and, used to London, I put my hand on the handle of the back door. The driver looked up at me and said, 'Do I bleedin' stink then?' You sit in the front with the driver in Sydney, which I am always happy to do anyway, but in a Test series it's, 'You bleedin' Poms haven't got a chance, we'll mop you, mate.'

Yes, there can be no greater pleasure than a tour of Australia with a winning English side, especially if they have lost the first Test match, oh glorious. They are not the world's greatest losers.

Yes they do melt away a bit. Mind you, they melt away all over the place, don't they? I have seen them melt away at Kent when they are not doing very well, in a much different style. Rather nicely spoken, sort of smiling style when things go well, but they melt away quietly.

But not like the Australians, Mike, no, you must admit, not like the Australians. Nobody gets so bitter as the Australians, and nobody has ever been on the receiving end of that more desperately than you, except perhaps Harold Larwood and Douglas Jardine. To go there and win is great but you can come back with scars on the soul.

Mind you, the biggest opposition and hostility was when we in fact lost the time after, because we won the year before and then the Packer players came back and we didn't agree to all the detail that they wanted. I seemed to be, to them, the person who made all the decisions as to what rules we played under and everything, and it was quite an interesting tour.

Did you ever do a braver, a better or calmer thing in your life than that? I must say I boiled with indignation for you and was overwhelmed with admiration that you could put up with it. I couldn't have put up with it. Perhaps you couldn't buy a machine-gun.

England v Australia, Third Test, Melbourne, 1980. Australians welcome Brearley

The famous Sydney crowd, January 1983

I met Bob Hawke there towards the end of the tour who is now the Prime Minister. He told me that he thought I didn't quite handle the Ockers as well as I might have and that they weren't all as bad as I probably thought. In fact quite a lot of them voted for him, he said!

The Ocker is an unfortunate symbol that too many of them have adopted. People like Dennis Lilley and Rod Marsh almost welcome the concept of the Ocker image. It's not nice.

Rowe caught Ian Chappell bowled Thomson, Third Test, Australia v West Indies, Melbourne, 1975. This was Ian Chappell's 100th Test catch

73

I take Marsh out of that category. I'd put Ian Chappell in, but I would take Marsh out. About Marsh, occasionally he got angry if he thought they had been done, but generally speaking he never appealed unless he thought it was out.

I used to get great fun out of him, because somebody would say, 'Ah, you're being tough again, Rod,' and I'd say, 'He is not tough, he is a dear, nice, sweet teddy, he's a cuddly teddy bear.' *'Get away'*, he would say. This is the one thing he couldn't stand. He would take almost everything else, but not being described as a nice cuddly bear of a man.

I suppose not many people would, really.

No, let's let Rod off if only on account of that wonderful calling back when he said not out.

Randall[18]? I believe Greg Chappell was so fed up he went off to fine leg for a couple of overs, took no part in the running of the match. Yes, I think Rod Marsh is alright. He bristles, doesn't he, he doesn't shave and he bristles on the field. There is a nice story of him with Derek Randall who was coming in to bat one day, I think it was in England in a Test match, and saying – they never could understand Randall, a lot of people can't understand him, and the Australians could understand him less than the rest of us – 'Ey up, Marshie, how you going then?' and Rod Marsh didn't say anything. 'Are we not chatting then today?' asks Randall, and eventually Marsh says, 'What do you think this is, a garden party?' But he was all right and off the field quiet and a very warm man.

Yes, I have known some splendid Australians, especially the nice tame ones who have settled in England like Neil Hawke. Bill Alley is still here, always is that elegant, dignified, Sydney sider! What a good player! What a loss he was to the first-class game for years, a top class player; yes, they do make me laugh sometimes, but not always. Sometimes they make me very cross. They don't lose well.

Then again it was my experience that Rod Marsh would be the first at the end of a Test Match that we had won to come and shake everyone by the hand and say 'Well played'.

What I always remember, and I am not always proud of our reactions, especially the reactions of our football supporters,

[18] Notts and England

Rodney Marsh claims the wicket of Geoffrey Boycott, Edgbaston, 1980

Rodney Marsh can only watch on this occasion as Derek Randall compiles a brilliant
century in the Centenary Test, Melbourne, 1977

but in 1948 when Bradman's side rolled over us like a steamroller and there was the outside chance of a win at Headingly, and we missed it, dropping two crucial catches. And then they came to the Oval, and they won. And the cheers, the farewell for Bradman and the cheers for the side were so generous, I have never been prouder of an English crowd of any sort in my life, and they haven't often shown *us* that kind of generosity. But it's hard if you have been trying and you are competitive and you are a good performer, it is very, very hard to lose easily.

I didn't find the Australian players bad; the public perhaps, but not the players. What about post-war sides?

A great side of 1948.

The best side, do you think?

I think, yes. The batting, you see, was so massive. You realise a player as good as Bill Brown I think only got into one or two Tests in 1948?

The 1948 Australian tourists at Worcester:
left-right: standing: I W Johnson, A R Morris, E R H Toshack, K R Miller, D Tallon,
R Lindwall, R N Harvey
seated: W A Brown, A L Hassett, D G Bradman, C L McCool, S G Barnes

There was Lindwall, Miller, Sam Loxton, Doug Ring, Bill Johnston, perhaps the most underestimated of all post-war cricketers, a superb left-arm bowler. Used to get Cyril Washbrook[19] into terrible trouble with this thing that floated away from him. And Siddy Barnes, Morris who was coming in first with him, the first time we had seen him, a massive left-hander; and the Don. He didn't start as well as he had done and you always felt somebody might get him out in the first over, but after that he was still the great killer of old, and a wiser and more mellow man, and less worried about his own image because now he was accepted. Yet he'd come so close, you see, in 1946/7 to leaving the game, and perhaps it all turned on one catch decision out there.

I didn't know about this, John. What happened?

Well, he was given not out when it was believed he was caught at slip and he went on to make a hundred. Previously in the season he'd done very little and it was thought that if he'd been given out then he would have gone. Thank goodness he didn't, because a whole generation of people in England, who'd never seen him before, had that infinite pleasure, such a great pleasure. There's never been anyone to my mind who was a more certain punisher of the bad ball or even the not very good one. When they made 721 in a day against Essex – I think it was less than a day actually – they made Tom Pearce a member of the Purchasers[20] for being the first county captain to get the Australians out in a day! 721!

When Miller gave up, the Don was in just before lunch, and Tom decided to try Frank Vigar who bowled fairly average leg-breaks, below average in fact. Six balls of the over the Don set off down the track. Six times he hit him and the sixth time before the ball hit mid-off's hands the Don had dropped his batting glove as he'd got five fours off the over and this one had hit a fieldsman and he couldn't forgive himself.

And a good captain. Then, of course, subsequently, one of the wisest of all the elders of cricket. They pulled his leg and joked about him when he was young, but he had the last laugh.

He's pretty shrewd, isn't he?

Very shrewd, and something perhaps a bit more than shrewd nowadays. Always shrewd, always sharp, but now wise as

---

[19] Lancashire and England
[20] A charity-raising club, largely for cricketers

The incomparable Don Bradman, 1948

well. Sage, perhaps, is the word.

Miller and Lindwall, you know. I suppose they were the exact parallel of Gregory and McDonald. As French mothers used to scare their children with rhymes about Marlborough, so they almost used to frighten children in England with

Lindwall (*left*) and Miller, 1953

stories of Gregory and McDonald in 1921 and Miller and Lindwall in 1948. They really were the ogres of the game.

I can remember 1948 being supposedly the season of English euphoria and fun because in 1947, the season of Compton and Edrich,[21] England had beaten South Africa. Then suddenly, in 1948, Miller and Lindwall!

You'd get a Test ground absolutely crammed full and they'd come on and you'd see somebody who had been to get a beer coming back from the bar with the glass in his hand. Miller or Lindwall would move in to bowl and he'd stand as if frozen and you would see a whole ground absolutely motionless and utterly silent and this great swish of the Rolls-Royce of Lindwall sweeping in, or Keith coming up and bouncing them.

Oh, again you see, one's impressionable, that's what I was going to say, impressionable as all that. I was young, but it was a most wonderful season even though we were beaten.

Yes, you've told me about the generosity of the crowds to the Australians at that time.

80   [21] Both Middlesex and England

Miller in action, Worcestershire v Australia, Worcester, 1948

They did admire them; they knew what was good. That's the thing – to have known the best and to have known it for the best, to have recognised it, to have recognised how wonderful and superb it all was. And you know, this happens to you and you're just grateful all your days that you had the luck to see it.

Lindwall in action, 1953

I suppose that people who saw the series of 1981, who saw Ian Botham turn those Test Matches, are going to remember that all their days. They'll bore their kids to death, won't they, and the children won't believe what they did!

What about the West Indies since the war? Because there was first of all the three Ws, Worrell, Weekes and Walcott, then Ramadhin and Valentine. And recently their great sides with the fast bowling, and Viv Richards and so on.

Yes, and earlier of course there was Constantine. I suppose if you're going to be certain of any superlative in the history of cricket it's got to be that Constantine was the greatest fields-man of all time.

Learie Constantine sits at the front of the West Indies tourists of 1923

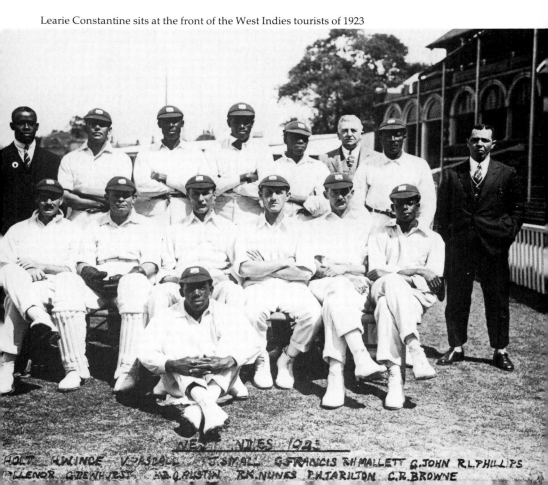

And George Headley you'd probably say was the greatest back-foot player of all time, because I don't think anybody ever saw him play forward when he could play back. But 1950, of course, Ram and Val made a wonderful pair of spinners. When people talk about them in that series, you know, some of them forget Weekes, Worrell and Walcott, and not many countries ever brought as strong batting as that here.

I shall always remember that great West Indian win of 1950, Ramadin and Valentine in that. An originally stunned English public – and by heaven they were stunned, they couldn't have read the reports that West Indies had won so many series over

The three Ws: Frank Worrell, May 1950

84

there, although they had never won any here – I'm not sure, but moved as the West Indian spectators were, I'm not sure that in many respects those English spectators, once they had got over their surprise, weren't even more impressed.

They were a funny couple weren't they? Those two on the boat over – the rest of the team spent most of the time teaching them to sign their autograph. It didn't matter whether they could bowl or not, but in England they had got to sign their autographs!

Garfield Sobers said to Charlie Davis when he came over, 'Charlie, if you are going to be an English County Cricketer,

Everton Weekes

you won't qualify until you have eaten half a ton of lettuce.'
You must have had enough county ground lunches to know
how deadly true that is!

Not true at Lord's though.

No. Lord's are very good. I always like that story of Ted Dexter
when he was Test captain saying why do we always have to
give them hot tomato soup in hot weather? Why don't we give
them a nice well-chilled consommé? So they duly served this
and the Australians to a man complained that the soup was
cold! I always cherished that one.

Clive Walcott

Anyway, then of course there were these ponderous sides of recent years. I think Clive Lloyd, you know, deserves a great big credit mark for handling those sides. They weren't always easy to handle and he's been the ultimate pragmatist, hasn't he? He said, if you do well with a pair of fast bowlers, you ought to do twice as well with four fast bowlers. Nobody else, of course, has ever had four really fast bowlers. But that was shattering. I don't like what he's done to the over rate, but he didn't start it, did he?

No, and he had one of the most beautiful bowlers I've ever seen, Michael Holding, and one of the quietest.

Yes, the umpires used to look round because they didn't hear him coming.

The modern West Indies in celebratory mood at the Oval, 1976.
England's Tony Greig has just been bowled by Michael Holding.
Captain Clive Lloyd is second from right

Mike Brearley faces up to Michael Holding

Yes, and the non-strike batsman. The only thing you'd hear was the final foot coming down, the left foot, but he ran in like a sprinter, which he was.

So did Ted McDonald, of course, but yes, Holding was a wonderful spectacle. Andy Roberts, perhaps one of the shrewdest and most controlled of fast bowlers. Your man, Wayne Daniel, very unlucky not to be in, wasn't he?

He's still only twenty-five, Wayne.

What a giant, and what an effect life in England has had on him, hasn't it?

Wayne Daniel

Yes, Well, he's one of the nicest of men. As somebody told me – something that I hadn't noticed – that he saw himself as a sort of father figure for all the young black players of West Indian origin on the staff. And so he would just have a word here or there, just keep an eye on them, make sure that they behaved right, a sort of junior senior pro.

And if he had difficulty, well, he could always go in and deliver them a bouncer.

Yes, that's right, in the nets!

Then Viv Richards. Kanhai, superb – in a way a historically underestimated player, I suppose. And their fielding vastly improved, above all. Although they were beating England in the West Indies between the two wars, I think they were overawed in England and they expected to lose and they did.

I think Worrell had something to do with that change.

An immense amount. Yes, a considerable amount. The first West Indian statesman cricketer.

I happened to see what you obviously saw, because you were working and describing it, the last day of the Lord's Test in 1963 when Wes Hall bowled from one o'clock until six o'clock and it got darker and darker and eventually England were six runs short and Colin Cowdrey[22] came in with his plaster on his arm.

Yes.

Brian Close[23] had seventeen bruises on his ribs where he let the ball hit him, but I remember Frank Worrell, how you were always conscious of his presence on the field as a quiet influence on people who were almost beside themselves with excitement, as we were in the audience. But Wes, I mean when Brian Close came down the wicket to him, Wes nearly went apoplectic and Frank just quietly calmed him.

And I said to Wes afterwards, 'What did Frank say to you in that last over?' He said, 'He come up to me and he said, "You bowl a no-ball, Wes, and I'll thump you!"'

Yes, yes, a wonderful day.

[22] Kent and England
[23] Yorkshire and England

Viv Richards, a new victorious captain of the West Indies

But the county game has been the part of cricket that you've most loved, hasn't it? Even more than Tests.

Yes. Much better than Test cricket. Test cricket's all very well as a spectacle and all that, but I love a county game – you know, perhaps at Glastonbury or Horsham or Neath or Ebbw Vale, where you can hear the players talking to each other. You used to be able to hear Wooller cursing the batsman and once I remember seeing Haydon Davies hit six balls into the river at Ebbw Vale in a single innings. And you feel somehow close to the players. This is where you get a bond with county cricket, and this is where they look so right and so good there.

You never know a footballer really by what he does on the field, or only very rarely. You might with a chap like Tommy Harmer,[24] or someone like that, but as a general rule he isn't doing his thing. He's doing what the manager tells him to do and it's an hour and a half and when he's done it he goes, and you've felt no great rapport with him.

With a cricketer, you watch him for three days and you've got to see the kind of man he is. He's got to reveal himself – especially a batsman. Oh, I don't know, and the bowler as well, certainly the wicket-keeper. Perhaps this is why there have been so few bad people in county cricket, because if you're bad you can't conceal it – I think. There have been a few who weren't quite nice and who weren't always liked, but fewer than in any other field of sport I believe.

I think this also demonstrates why there's been so much more of a cricket literature than there has for other sports. I mean, there's the time and the different aspects of character that are revealed in the context of the play.

[24] Spurs

More to appreciate and more to understand. Funnily enough, of course, nobody really tried to express it until Cardus did in the early twenties. And people take him for granted now. They find it difficult to realise what an absolute revelation it was, this writing about these slightly larger-than-life characters. And yet they were true to type. It was almost like a morality play – he was writing of types rather than actual people – and yet they were so *right*. And you went and saw them and you found yourself almost using Cardus's words when you told somebody about it afterwards. A great thing he did. I doubt if there was ever a writer with such a wide range of understanding.

John, all of your life you've lived in the south of England, and your first loves were Hampshire and then Sussex. What about the great Yorkshire sides of the thirties?

There's a story I love about that. The people, after a cricket match, gather in a nearby pub and they're talking about cricket and somebody says to one lad, 'Where do you come from, then?' He says, 'Oh, I come from Cornwall. Not a first-class county, we're not really involved. In fact, we don't give a damn who beats Yorkshire!'

You know the great thing the counties used to remember was when they beat Yorkshire. I remember being with Reg Perks[25] and Peter Jackson,[26] when Worcester beat them in either 1930 or '31, at Stourbridge, I think, and Charles Lyttelton threw this spectacular party and took everybody to the funfair, and gave them all dinner because they'd beaten Yorkshire.

When Hampshire beat 'em it used to be a state occasion. It didn't happen very often. Between the two wars, they were so strong that they filled the rest of the country with awe.

[25] Worcestershire and England
[26] Worcestershire

I remember having a talk with Maurice Leyland[27] once and saying I reckoned at one time, between the two wars, Hampshire had very nearly as strong a side as Yorkshire.

'Don't talk daft,' said Maurice.

'Well, now,' I added, 'first of all we'll compare Lionel Tennyson with your captain.'

'Nay, I don't count captain in t'Yorkshire side,' said Maurice. 'We do it with ten.'

And they did, didn't they?

Yes, they did it constantly. Very old story of Yorkshire batting at Lord's and Wilfred Rhodes chatting away to somebody in the dressing-room appearing not to watch the play. It had been raining and the sun was shining, and all of a sudden a ball jumped off a length. Wilfred turned round and said, 'Call 'em in, captain,' and went on with his conversation. Declared as soon as the ball began to turn and Wilfred was ready to go on. But they were legendary. They were terrific, weren't they? Full of the lore of the game, and it's been a shame actually, their post-war decline, though it's not a total post-war decline because they did have their successes, didn't they, just after the war?

And again in the sixties. And it was still . . . it was still a different feeling to be playing against Yorkshire and still a pleasure in beating them even if one beat them more often than before. There was identity there, a real feeling you were entering a territory.

It was a place where cricket belonged.

Right: Wilfred Rhodes, 1927

[27] Yorkshire and England

We got to know each other partly at the time of the d'Oliveira affair, as it could be called, in 1969. Of course your experience in South Africa, your contacts in South Africa, went a long way back before that, didn't they?

Yes, I went in 1948/9 and I was desperately shocked by what I saw there. I never dreamt that these things went on. I had heard lip-service paid to the awfulness, but you see this was just the time when the first nationalist government of Doctor Malan was returned, and I saw and heard some quite terrible things about what happened to ordinary black people. I didn't know what to do. I still haven't really done much about it. I haven't done as much as I ought to have done.

You see, it's so easy, especially for English people, especially for cricketers, to go to South Africa and not see what goes on, because it is not flaunted, it is not pushed under their noses. Sometimes you would find great difficulty in finding a taxi driver who would take you to these compounds.

I thought perhaps I had done something when I helped bring Basil d'Oliveira into this country and I think that did do something that perhaps we can't see. It must have convinced a lot of people that their cause wasn't quite lost. If one could do it, in a way it stood for them all. But then you see there has been such a clampdown since, certainly on liberal thinking and a certain amount of increased repression. Old Jan Smuts was so clever, he used to give them a fresh liberty every year; it would have taken two hundred years for them to be really free. But he didn't impose fresh restrictions and fresh repressions, as the nationalist government has done since, and this is distressing, it's distressing to think about it.

I don't know what the answer is, except perhaps the most appalling one of all, which one can't lay one's tongue to. But it is going to be explosive in the end, I feel all too sure of that.

John, I know you thought it was an important thing you did to help get Basil d'Oliveira to come to England. How did that happen?

Well, out of the blue I got this letter from a young man, beautifully written in green ink, terribly courteous, saying how much he loved cricket and how much he would like to learn to qualify to be a coach in England so that he could go back to South Africa and teach his own people. I thought I never heard of anything much more hopeless, really. But there was such charm in the letters, and I went on replying to them to see what we could work out.

Basil d'Oliveira

Basil d'Oliveira

In the end I said, well, how good a player are you, because if you want to come here probably your only hope is as a player. Then he sent me some pretty remarkable statistics of his performances. He had gone as high as he could in cricket for a Cape coloured, and I really began to give up hope. People just couldn't see. If I said, look this chap made 286, with so many sixes, they said it must have been an absolutely plumb wicket. And if in the same match he took 6 for 16, they said oh, it must have been an awful wicket, it must have been a bad batting side – they wanted it both ways.

Well, then Alan Oakman[28] and Pete Sainsbury[29] and Jim Gray[30] played in a mixed match and saw him play. They came back, and I said, what is he like? They said, he is a very, very gifted player. Quite talented, and crude, but still first class. Still he never could get anywhere.

But John Kay helped me immensely – *Manchester Evening News* and the Manchester League expert and player – when all of a sudden he told me that his club Middleton had got rid of Gilchrist and had been trying rather secretively to sign on Wes Hall and, at the last minute, Wes had let them down. So John rang me up and said, 'Look, if your chap wants a job, he can come.' He suggested a wage which was very low, but this had been going on for six years and eventually I wrote and said, 'Look, your chance has come, I don't think it will ever come again. I know the money is not good, but if you want to come, say yes to this and come.'

He decided to accept and they had a whip-round in the local village and he came. He made a terrible start, poor kid, couldn't get a run for a month. He had never seen these slow, sodden, muddy wickets. Then all of a sudden everything came good for him at the end of May. He actually finished with more runs than Garfield Sobers in his first season.

And I mean, if you had seen, I almost wept, his amazement at sitting down to eat with white people in the dining-car of the train and at the airport and so on. Yet he kept utter and absolute dignity and good nature, and I think, through all the troubles, probably behaved better than anybody else. And as you know, he became a British citizen, he played for England, shook hands with the Queen, and he never made a fool of himself, which would have been so easy. But I just think he played it with infinite dignity.

What I think was important about Basil is that he gave hope to his own people, millions of them. It isn't going to happen to them, but they knew there was hope. It was possible, if not for

---

[28] Sussex and England
[29] Hampshire
[30] Hampshire

them, for their children, or their children's children, and this was the important thing about his coming here. To prove that bondage was not inevitable.

He was not only dignified, he was actually reticent, wasn't he? And I remember feeling, I wished he would come out with what he felt about it and I had no idea until recently, after the big row had subsided, just how passionately he always felt.

Oh, he did in private and people used to try and goad him into exploding and he wouldn't. This was where the dignity was immense, because anybody who has lived under that kind of bondage has got to hate it, and he never showed the hate.

From the cricket point of view, how can you see Test cricket surviving? It's a slender thread all the time, isn't it?

Desperately so, because of the men who will do anything for money, even a little money. But this Gleneagles agreement was voluntarily entered into and I think one must stand by it and if we do I am also sure that that is the likeliest way of producing an improvement.

It has produced some minor improvements in the last ten or twelve years.

That is the only thing that has reversed the tide.

And it's very questionable how far the tide has been reversed, but it has been pushed back a little bit in some areas.

You wouldn't want to go again?

I was on the last MCC tour there, as a young hopeful who did all right for a while, but then had a terrible end to the tour from a cricket point of view. But I stayed on and went around and saw whatever I could see of the Bantustans and the Transkei and met politicians of different views, and like you, I was appalled. It was much worse than I had imagined, and that was what made me feel that I didn't want to have anything to do with it again. I didn't know how to make any difference, but I didn't want to have any more to do with it than I had to.
  The other thing I felt was that we are trying in this country to be multiracial in every way, and it's also a symbol for black people in

Great Britain that we don't put South Africa and dealing with South Africa first.

Yes, I am sure that is absolutely true, because one of the things that few people ever mention is the great necessity in an increasingly multiracial society to convince of our sincerity. If this were done, there would be far less doubt and far less anxiety on the part of the people coming in, especially from the West Indies, as to where we do stand.

To say you must keep politics out of sport is ludicrous, because politics control everything we do, whether it's our attitude to sport, the money that is made available for sport, or literature, what we eat, what we drink, what is prohibited from coming into the country, absolutely everything we do is controlled by politics. It's impossible to say that sport isn't or can't be; it must be, it always is.

The other big thing that has split cricketers and cricket and looked as though it might really damage Test cricket permanently was the Packer affair, which started just after the Centenary Test in 1977.

You and I saw eye to eye, I think, on that right from the start in that we recognised that the split must not be perpetuated. As you know there was this damaging court case, but it was apparent, to me at least, from the start that if they divided cricket into two worlds, the Packer world and the anti-Packer world, the whole game was going to collapse. You would get competing Test Matches, and that had to be avoided at all costs.

Now, first of all I think that what many people didn't realise was that this was economically inevitable because cricket had not paid its players enough money. It's as simple as that. Therefore the way was open for a very long time. As the judge said, the only surprising thing about it was that it hadn't happened earlier. You see, I think it could all have been sorted

Benson and Hedges World Series Cricket match, Australia v England at Sydney.
Willis has been caught by Marsh off Chappell and Australian victory is almost certain

out very smoothly but for a clash of hostile personalities. The attitude of the Australian Board of Control was really truculent; one would never have thought that they were eventually going to give in, come and eat out of Packer's hand. Packer runs Australian cricket now and the Board of Control is a joke. Our people headed that off, but I think it could all have been dealt with quite easily if Packer had been a more sympathetic type. He wanted to be the boss; he wanted to run everything; and he didn't want to negotiate except on his terms. This made it very difficult.

I remember going to see him. First of all I couldn't resist pulling his leg, but then I realised how I had to keep my lip right under my teeth and above all not to lose my temper. It was still very difficult; there were a lot of players who felt terribly strongly on both sides. Either they wanted to be there because of the good money or they saw the structure of the game as they knew it being threatened by the people who were taking the money, and wanted to ban them and Packer as well. But I think the best thing the Cricketers' Association ever did was to make common cause within itself on the issue and to help the others to make common cause as well. That is when the Association really grew up and became responsible. Perhaps it's unjust to say it – it claims too much – but I think we did more to heal the rift than anybody else.

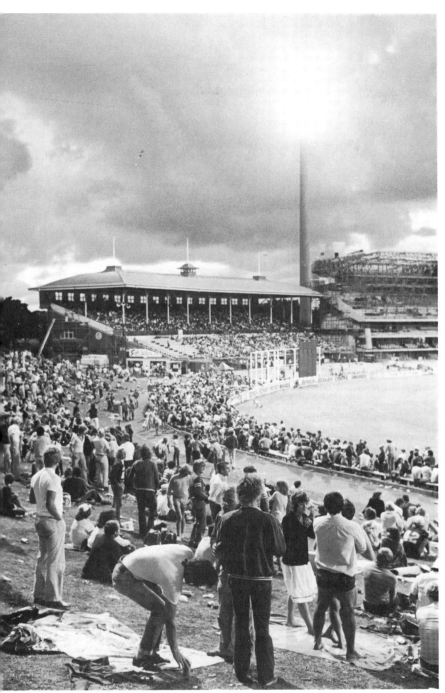

With the arrival of World Series Cricket, floodlit matches became a regular feature of Australian sporting life, 1983

John, twice you have stood for Parliament as a Liberal candidate. Tell us about that.

Well, I felt I owed this to my mother and father. I was asked to stand and I went and did it. I had a nice agent, Norman Hoddell, who did all sorts of calculations; we had gone from a forfeited deposit up thirty-three and a third and up thirty-three and a third, or something like this, and he suddenly said, "You know, in two elections you will be in". This frightened me to death and, because my family wouldn't have eaten or been educated, I wasn't sure that I wanted to be a full-time politician, that I was that sort of person. On the other hand, I was very deeply devoted to the Liberals, particularly at that time and especially to the Party leader, Jo Grimond, who I take to be one of the greatest men I ever knew.

So they came to me one day and said would I fight North Dorset, because if I would Donald Wade would go to the Lords and I would become Chief Whip, which under Jo Grimond would have been very pleasant indeed. So I thought very deeply about this. They wanted me to fight North Dorset – Frank Byers had won it two elections before and narrowly lost it. Then Winkie Portman had fought it in the most elegant fashion in a Rolls-Royce and a pair of carpet slippers and lost it because that didn't exactly appeal to the Dorset rustics.

I thought a long time about this and I decided again I probably wasn't good enough. The funny thing is, you see, Wade did go to the Lords and they made Jeremy Thorpe Chief Whip. Then Jo pulled out and Jeremy became party leader. I can only assume – I sometimes wake in the night with my hair almost standing on end – if that had happened I might have become leader of the Liberal party instead of Jeremy Thorpe, who, whatever people may have said afterwards, was hailed with fairly great delight when it happened. And this convinced me. I thought, I couldn't have done it, I wouldn't have made a party leader, any more than I could hire or fire. I wouldn't have made a party leader.

104

John Arlott as the Liberal candidate for Epping, 1955

But it's exciting. It's a most unmodest thing to be a Parliamentary candidate, you are exaggerated far beyond your abilities, capabilities or merits, but it is immensely stimulating.

You say you don't think you could have done it. You are implying that it's the degree of sentiment and the difficulty of being hard enough, or maybe ambitious enough, controlling enough, that would have been the problem for you?

I'm certainly not ambitious enough, not hard enough, that's absolutely certain. I'm a very dangerous sentimentalist, really. I think you have to be cleverer and harder than I am to be a political leader, but I must say to have fought one election campaign as one would have been terrific.

And Jo Grimond had this quality?

Jo Grimond, 1960

Yes, he had, although I think perhaps he is not all that hard or all that competitive and more of an idealist. When he went away to think out politics for himself, I wrote and said how much I was going to miss him and if ever he came back I was his man. I think a lot of people felt that.

But you had a great admiration also for his perceptiveness and intellect, didn't you?

Yes. For example, the story of the morning of Suez. The morning the Suez news broke, I was in a *News Chronicle* conference when the phone call came through on the editor's telephone. A call for Arlott, the humblest member of the gang, would I go to Frank Owen's flat for a meeting of the Liberal party executive?

I went over and I sat down next to Jo, and I said,

'Jo, this is the end of us.'

'Tell me,' he said, 'by what complicated process did you reach that conclusion?'

'It's the end of Eden.'

'That's certain,' he said.

'That means Butler will come in,' I added. 'Butler is the most liberal of all the Tories and that will shoot the ground from under our feet.'

'If it happens,' he said, 'but it won't happen.'

'Oh?'

'Macmillan.'

'Macmillan?' I asked.

'Oh, yes,' he said, 'the most Machiavellian, probably the most brilliant member of the House. He can unite the extreme right and extreme left of the Conservative party. He will have fresh ideas, fresh things to say, and if he makes mistakes other people will resign as a result of it.'

My word, that was pretty astute on the morning of Suez. That's how good Jo was and is. It may be that he is happier at the University of Kent, more use there, but I think he might have done British politics an immense amount of good.

And there was a tradition of political interest in the family?

Yes, both my grandfathers were furious Gladstonians. One of them looked like Gladstone and the other looked the very opposite, but, yes, they were both Liberals, both trade union-ists, trade-union idealists. My father and my grandfather built NALGO in Basingstoke under threats from the borough sur-veyor. 'I'll see you two out of work and on the dole,' he said. Well, it didn't happen, but it was a nasty sort of threat to make. I don't know what they would think of some of the tactics nowadays but they brought me up a trade unionist idealist.

But also independent of the mainstream trade unionist political affiliation?

Yes. Always been Liberal. But the Liberals, of course, were

John Arlott in his campaigning days, 1955

the first people to give the trade unionists any protection, and they do have an extremely good record there.

You are still an active supporter of the Liberal/SDP Alliance?

I am still president of the Winchester constituency, although I ought not to be since I no longer live in it. I ought to be released or pushed out on my ear. But I am a most enthusiastic supporter of the Liberal/SDP Alliance and I just pray that the Liberals won't back out and break the Alliance or that the others don't, for that matter. Yes, deeply involved, but too old to be active.

Was there any appeal in its being a party that doesn't look like winning an election?

No, because you never believe that if you are in it. The most idealistic of parties, with wonderful support. There weren't so many of them, but by Heaven they were decent people and you really felt this. I have never been in anything that was remotely a dirty campaign as far as the Liberals were concerned.

Were you president of the Young Liberals at one time?

Yes, and a member of the executive. All sorts of things. My trouble is that as soon as I become mildly involved, I become deeply involved.

And people want you to be?

I don't know about that, but they find they have got me.

What about political dissent? Where do you think political dissent or civil disobedience is allowable and should be recommended?

Oh, peaceful demonstration has got to be good. I worked long enough for the Eastern Service of the BBC doing poetry programmes and mixing with Indians and reading about Gandhi to know that. I did the memorial programme on the day Gandhi died, but only because I was the only person in the office when the news came through. His non-violent contribution to changing the shape of the world was desperately important. I don't think he was quite the innocent that some people pretend, though. He was quite a shrewd man, but on the other hand I think he was fundamentally innocent, and I think he was sincere and he was honest.

In a BBC Overseas Service studio with the 1946 Indian tourists

Were you a supporter of Gandhi while it was happening? Did you believe in what he was saying?

Yes, he was an immense person; with lack of force he achieved more than most people by force, in shaping the world.

I remember talking to Vijay Merchant once, the Indian batsman, and saying that Britain must yield them self-government.

'Of course,' he said, 'they can't afford not to.'

'But if they do you will have a civil war.'

'That is quite possible,' he replied. 'But was there not, or am I incorrect, an Englishman named Cromwell who started a civil war before you worked out your political destiny?'

What could I say to that?

Nehru I thought, too, was a considerable man. They have produced great statesmen.

You have been to India, haven't you?

Yes.

Did you like it?

It's rather like the curate's egg. I liked Delhi, I hated Calcutta. I did not like Bombay, but New Delhi I thought was a city of infinite majesty, dignity, but it has its troubles. I couldn't face them. Thank goodness I'm not involved in politics and responsible for them.

Are you sanguine about the world's prospects of survival?

I wish I could say yes, but you see I'm a pessimist. I am worried. I think there are too many old men in politics who don't think far enough into the future, who wouldn't mind a war. And anybody who wouldn't mind a war in these days to my mind is beyond the pale.

John, you have collected a great many things in your life. What is the source of it and what have you been interested in collecting?

I have collected many things. I am a cross between a magpie and a squirrel, an odd hybrid, but you tell me, you're the psychoanalyst, what makes a collector?

I don't know. I suppose you want to make something part of yourself, the thing that you are most interested in part of yourself. I haven't collected things myself.

No, you are too clear minded.

But there are many things that people collect that I don't, postage stamps and things like this. I collect things that I like and I can enjoy. I don't collect things to put away in files. I collect furniture because I like to live with it. Good furniture, not expensive, but pieces of furniture that I find in junk-shops and buy and bring home. Books, books all my life, fiction, novels, a long collection of novels, then history. Then all these books illustrated with aquatint plates, not just the colour plates but the sepia aquatint, which I take to be the purest.

What is it?

John Arlott at home in Alderney, 1981

Oh dear, I could bore your head off. You get a copper plate, and put resin on it, and heat it until the resin runs across the plate. Then you scrape away an area of it and then dip it in the acid and then take it out. Then you scrape away another area, then another, then another, and then another. The area that you scraped away first will get six dippings in the acid and the others will get a declining number of dippings, so that you get all these different shades of one colour when you ultimately put the ink on and the depth of the ink comes out.

It was the great method of English illustration. I believe the finest form of illustration there has ever been in the history of the world. It existed from about 1775 to 1825 when unhappily it was superseded by the lithograph. I don't deplore the lithograph, but there was room for the two together. But aquatint was harder work, much harder work.

John Piper did a splendid series of Brighton aquatints in the 1930s but there has been no other comparable English work since about 1837 and substantially it ended in 1825. But they are the most handsome illustrated books there have ever been. I was lucky to get after them before the prices went up because there are only a few worthwhile titles that I haven't got now and I couldn't possibly afford to buy them if they turned up. But aquatints are my best collection in terms of importance.

Then there are the cricket reference books. Wine and gastronomy, not so much cookery books, although I do acquire them if only as a way of pretending to my wife that I know best. General sport, a fair collection of biographies and a lot of modern poetry. I mean a fair amount of classical poetry, but most of all modern poetry. People like Andrew Young, Dylan Thomas, John Betjeman, the three most important, all of whom I knew, plus Thomas Hardy, whom I didn't.

I never know whether to call Hardy a great poet or a great novelist or both. I suppose he must be the greatest of all English novelists. Yes, I don't think there is a doubt. *Jude the Obscure* in particular.

I read *Jude* first in Austria, just after the war, in Graz in a hotel looking down over that river where the rapids tumble under the bridge, and I got to that passage where the boy opens the wardrobe and sees the bodies, the hanging bodies. I dropped the book on the bedroom floor and I went out and pressed the lift button. There was nothing there, so I ran down seven flights of stairs because I was so frightened. I had

Thomas Hardy,
1840–1928

John Arlott reads
a book of poems
by Andrew
Young, his first
major influence,
c 1948

to speak to somebody to get the terror out of my soul. You can talk about suspension of disbelief in reading or in a play or a film, but I have never known anything like that. It obsessed me with fear; no, not fear, horror.

Hardy was a mean mercenary little man, wasn't he? He was the highest paid writer of his day. He wrote these clever serials because he could leave you in suspense every week or every month, whichever was appropriate. Yet you see this terrific command, this knowledge, this earthy understanding. All right, perhaps it's because I am a peasant from the South Country, a peasant man. I know about the way the men worked and the women suffered, I know about that, but still it's so true, I believe it would be valid for anybody in the world.

It was amazing when I first went to Japan. I went to see Edmund Blunden, who was then a professor of English literature in Japan. He said, will you come and talk to my Japanese students and do your South Country accent and read Hardy to them so they will know what Hardy sounded like? And this was quite amazing, this great expanse of Japanese faces, and their immense enthusiasm. They were terrific: I have a splendid book on Hardy completely in Japanese!

He was an immensely great man, but there are so many rather sad stories about him. He was trained as an architect originally of course, and when he was the wealthiest author in the world, he built himself a house at Max Gate, without a bathroom. And once the housemaid went in and she found Hardy raking the coals out of the fire and putting them into the fireplace to save them for the next day because it wasn't as cold as he had thought it was going to be.

Yet the touch of the master. You see I think you find if you meet great people, not that they are your friends, but if you just have the privilege of being close to them or knowing them, how often you will find it's a question of, as Milton said about his blindness, which was a different matter, this single talent, 'lodged with me useless'; how everything, everything of them has gone into their great gift and their great capability and they are drained and inadequate as human beings. This so often happens. You go to the man who is the greatest in his field and find there is a human being who is tragically disappointing. I think it's one of the greatest disappointments you encounter in life, to find that the man who is great at the thing you admire is third-rate as a human.

You haven't talked about Dylan Thomas.

Dylan was a lovely man. Now Aneurin Talfan-Davies said in his book that seventy-five per cent of Dylan's broadcasts were done for me, and I adored Dylan. We were of an age. We had known one another for years and, when I got this poetry producing job, I used to get Dylan in to read. He'd be away and I'd get a letter from him saying, 'Dear John, very hard up, may I come and boom for you next week?' and Dylan would come and read like an angel. He would stand up there with the script, a dead cigarette hanging from the lip, swaying to the rhythm of it, and he would sting the words out as if they were water almost freezing in cold air, they were so clear and sharp and distinct. Dylan worked for me on and off for five years which was as long as I produced.

In a rehearsal studio for a radio production of *Henry IV*:
left-right around the table: Hugh Metcalfe, John Arlott, Preston Lockwood, George Robey, Robin Holmes, Dylan Thomas, R N Currey

And they tell you he was a drunk. He never, never, never did a broadcast drunk for me. He always appeared sober. I am willing to believe that if he was asked to do a talk at Radio Swansea at half past nine in the evening, he might have had a few during the day before he got there, but that is a different matter.

But there is the story of Roy Campbell who was his pal. This is one of the ancient stories of the BBC. It's too long to tell in full, but Roy was a great big, husky South African. He loved bullfighting, and he lived in Spain, and wrote poetry of such

Poet and occasionally less-than-perfect broadcaster, Roy Campbell, 1946

incredible delicacy and subtlety that you couldn't believe that this great big, wide-awake man had done it. Roy was given a sort of honorarium – talks producer in the BBC. They fairly soon discovered that he wasn't very good at producing talks, but what he could do was hold the stop-watch while a good actor read a short story, so he used to do that once a week.

Well, one night he had the evening short story to put out at 10.15. All he had to do was hold the script and get a news-reader to announce it, but he had forgotten to do that. Now, only Roy could have done it. He dashed over to The George in Great Portland Street where Dylan had been drinking since lunchtime, and he said, 'Dylan man, come on, I need an announcer to put this on.' So poor Dylan, led over willy-nilly, announced this story and it must have been the drunkenest utterance ever made on the BBC. Dylan was blamed and it wasn't Dylan's fault.

116

Some odd things used to happen. There was the time when Frances Campbell[31] came into an inheritance. It must have been about 1947, when fifty pounds was considered an inheritance. Frances decided that all her friends must come over to the Marlborough and drink on it.

Anyway, rather late in the evening, a gentleman who shall be nameless, a very considerable broadcaster, who at this time was a newsreader on Overseas, came up to me and said, 'Dear boy, I am to read the news to North America and the real trouble is I am sure I could read the news to North America, but I can't see the news to North America. What shall we do?' So with sublime drunken confidence I said, 'All right, I will read it.'

We went over and there was Aidan Thompson and I said, 'Will you give me the news?' We took it and we went down and I looked through it. He went out and sat at the control panel and as I was announced I saw his face, transfixed with horror, that I was going to fail him and ruin his career for ever, but I read the news and I came out on time.

Now, at that time Gilbert Harding was the BBC's representative in North America and we waited ten whole full days for his report. It came over and it said of 10.15 news on this particular day: 'Since the news was good, this was read with a quite unnecessarily lugubrious tone.' Which we thought was a very good get-away, it was only 'lugubrious'!

I am sure things like that don't happen nowadays.

It's more streamlined nowadays.

I suppose it is, but I suppose broadcasters are still pretty human. They were very human in my day, the whole life there was screamingly funny. People got jobs there; they came in to see you for a drink and would say, 'I am terribly hard up,' and – I did this twice – I'd say, well, come downstairs. One of them, far opposed to his wishes, became a newsreader in 1946, and he remained a newsreader until he retired, having never really wanted to be one.

[31] A BBC Programme Assistant

But he wanted the money.

He wanted the money, yes, and in the end he couldn't wriggle free. If he hears this he will grin all over his face and say, 'What did you do to me, Arlott?'

John Arlott, emergency narrator

You're a great collector, of people as well as things.

I collected people, friends, all my life. Books, furniture, junk, pottery. For years while I did *Any Questions?*, every Friday I used to go to the town we were broadcasting from, go round to the junk-shop and buy a named Staffordshire figure, for which I never paid more than a pound, and some of them are sixty, seventy, eighty pounds now. I have still got a fair collection. Sunderland pottery, engravings, water-colours, drawings, wine. I collected wine for years.

Of all your collections, if an exceptional penury came upon you, what would be the last thing you would sell?

I think just a few of the pictures because I can enjoy them all the time. Every day when I walk into a room, I don't forget they are there, I look at them. All those cricketers are so nostalgic to me. They bring back so many memories you see. They go from Constantine and Hobbs in the middle 1920s, right through to Botham today.

Constantine of course almost ruined me. I was fielding twelfth man for Hampshire at Worcester and they made a vast number of runs. Almost everybody in sight got a hundred, including a man named C. D. A. Pullan, who was a terrifically strong on-driver, and bruised my hands almost black. I was fielding mid-on and third man, which is about all I was fit for. Pataudi[32] made, as far as I can recall, 180, and at third man, if I was fine he played it square, if I was square he played it fine and he had me running backwards and forwards like a dog on a string.

Eventually he played one hard to the pavilion gate, and I had a long way to go. I knew I was never going to get round this ball. I don't know why it occurred to me, the least athletic of men, but I remembered Learie Constantine running over the ball, bending and picking it up between his legs as he went and throwing it in. So I did this. I got down to it all right and I got it in my hands. But I was going very, very fast, and there was all that water weed from the flooding in front of the Worcester pavilion. I felt my feet start to go.

Now my second appalling delusion was that I could turn a complete somersault, land on my shoulder blades and get up the other side, gangly and clumsy as I was. I did even succeed in that, but I shut my eyes with fear, drew my arm back and, as I opened my eyes, I saw the crowd in front of the Worcester pavilion opening like the Red Sea before the children of Israel: I was about to throw it in through the pavilion window! When I turned round to throw it the right way, Neil McCorkell the wicket-keeper was on his back with mirth, along with two other people, and they ran three from what should have been one to third man. At least I saved one. It wasn't a four.

That is how Constantine nearly ruined me.

It's amazing how if you play the game you can get the delusion for a

---

[32] The Nawab of Pataudi, Oxford, Worcestershire and India

Learie Constantine, fieldsman supreme

Dylan Thomas, 1946

moment that you are a great mover or a great player. I do that myself.

My large feet, and Lofty Herman's size-and-a-half too big crepes were my downfall, or overfall. Anyway, we were talking about collecting. Pictures, yes, pictures. They are such a motley lot. Osbert Lancaster, Flaxman, Ray Evans, Lowry, Beerbohm, unknown Japanese, Rowlandson; oh yes, Nicholas Bentley caricatures, several Osbert Lancasters, whom I enjoy immensely, John Piper.

Nearly all are of the human form in some way or another, sometimes distorted or caricatured.

Yes, the Beerbohms are superb, the cartoon of Thomas Hardy which everyone insists on regarding as Clem Attlee.

And Michael Ayrton's drawing of Dylan Thomas on the famous day when we went down the Thames together on the *Golden Eagle*, to write a piece called 'Day Out', I think it was, for the Forces Programme. Dear old Hugh Metcalfe was then stage manager of the Crazy Gang and he came back to take the *Golden Eagle* to Southend; that was the most fantastic day. We ate whelks, winkles, cockles, mussels, every kind of seafood in sight, and Dylan made absolutely certain of a vast array of alcohol. Michael drew Dylan on the way down, not on the way back!

That is the picture you have.

Yes. Some years later I went to the first day of a Michael Ayrton exhibition, saw the drawing and said I would have it. When he told me I didn't know how much it was, I still said I would have it. Then he told me that if I had asked how much it was he would have put the price up. Because I hadn't, he let me have it at cost. I am still delighted to have it.

Dylan was such a relishable, amusing man. He was glorious company, the poetic all-time extrovert. He was to alcohol what Houdini was to holding hands! I used to try to find out about it, because although I liked drink, I liked it within the bounds of reason. I said to him once, 'Tell me Dylan, why do you drink as much as you do?' He said, 'Do I drink as much as you do?' I said, 'Come on, you know you do.' 'Alright,' he said, 'I'll tell you then. I drink and I feel good. I go on drinking to stay feeling good and then I'm drunk.'

I asked him another time and he said, 'Because every time I

get drunk it's different.'

And that, I think, was the ultimate answer. He did have a compulsion not just to drink but to get drunk. But, after that, all the other . . . odd things they say about him in my experience were not true. I found him an absolutely lovable man. And as a reader of poetry he was without compare, although it had to be a great poem. I always remember we did a programme on Coventry Patmore, and we got him to read for it. Dylan said, 'I don't like this poem, it's not a nice poem.' It is cruel about women, he said, not a good poem. He said, 'I want the money but I can't read this poem.'

I said, all right, I would get somebody else to read it and he could read this, that and the other one. He said, 'They are not quite so bad. All right, I'll do that for the money. I don't like him, though.'

In those days poor Dylan was so hard up. The income tax had come down on him like a ton of bricks and everything he earned was paid to his agent, who had to make good both the arrears of income tax and current income tax and Dylan got about 10 per cent. That was why he went to America on the ultimate and fatal trip.

But I think everybody who really knew him in London knew he was a lovable man. He was a funny man, too, he would tell funny stories. He couldn't bear filthy stories, and he couldn't bear cruel stories. I heard him say to somebody, 'I suppose that's funny but it hurts me.'

He was another ancestor worshipper; he loved his mother and father. That wonderful story about getting his finger stuck in the bottle – he was a master of comic writing. The *Portrait of the Artist as a Young Dog* was extremely funny. He was a great comic man and *Under Milk Wood* is a very humanly funny play.

No, the modern people, poets above all, that I respect are Dylan, John Betjeman, Thomas Hardy and Andrew Young, and I suppose one of the poems that made the biggest impression on me in my life was by Andrew Young. I am not a good man for remembering poems, I don't learn them by rote but I remember it holding me, almost putting me in a block of ice. It is called *Passing the Graveyard*.

Passing the Graveyard

I see you did not try to save
The bouquet of white flowers I gave;
So fast they wither on your grave.

Why does it hurt the heart to think
Of that most bitter abrupt brink,
Where the low-shouldered coffins sink?

These living bodies that we wear
So change by every seventh year
That in a new dress we appear;

Limbs, spongy brain and slogging heart,
No part remains the selfsame part;
Like streams they stay yet still depart.

You slipped slow bodies in the past;
Why then should we be so aghast
You flung off the whole flesh at last?

Let him who loves you think instead
That like a woman who has wed
You undressed first and went to bed.

Andrew Young

Fantastic poet. Quiet, dour, Scots parson. All his life he worked on these poems and reduced them, polished them like a lapidarist. To my mind one of the three or four greatest poets of modern times. Taught me much, was very, very generous to me. He knew I would never make a poet, but he would never tell me so. I valued his friendship immensely.

Andrew Young

Let me ask you, are there decisions that you have actually regretted, things that you wish you had done?

Yes, that's a good question. There ought to be. I am trying to think because I have never thought of this before. What I suppose is that once I make a decision I accept it and I don't gripe if the dice fall the other way. I have been lucky, desperately lucky, in many ways. I am lucky on a few, a few of the important ones, to think that the cemetery keeper's boy was going to be a commentator, a poet, an author, even be conversed with by you. It's a pretty heavy thought, you know. It's one that you appreciate more than if you had been born into some kind of privilege. Sometimes you tell yourself you have done it yourself, but you know really that there is a vast element of luck in it, being in the right place at the right time, and doing the right thing that was wanted at the right time. I am sure there are fifty better commentators than me about the place, who are not doing commentary, but I was there when the chance happened.

Author at work: John Arlott at the Oval . . .

But I have a feeling also that you were quite ambitious to do well in something. You said about various things that at that point you saw you couldn't do any more and you weren't going to be good enough at it – wouldn't you say you wanted to do something really well?

. . . Mike Brearley in the slips. O'Keefe caught Brearley, bowled Underwood, Centenary Test, Melbourne, 1977

Yes, I did, but I wasn't looking for something to do well. I became interested in things and tried to do well at them, which, I think, is a different matter. I didn't want success at any price. I wanted to do what I have done, which is earn my living doing the things I have loved. You see, so few people are really happy in their work. Decent, nice, fundamentally contented chaps will tell you they are happy in their job, but they are not really. The job doesn't satisfy, doesn't please it doesn't make them terribly proud.

It is rarely you find people doing something that if they weren't doing it professionally they would do it as a hobby.

That's right, there aren't many of those.

We have both been fortunate in that way.

126

Yes, I think it might have taken a lot of persuasion to ask you to refuse the England captaincy, and it would have taken a lot to stop me becoming a commentator once I got the chance at it. Or a *Guardian* cricket correspondent, or almost all the other things I have ever been. I was desperately lucky, right time, right place.

But you didn't write the novel that you would have liked to have written. It is one thing you would have liked to have done, isn't it?

Yes, I would, and I think of Jim Pennethorne Hughes. All my life I have worked for and earned everything I ever got except that Jim Hughes, bless him, left me the contents of his cottage. He bought some lovely stuff and I know he wanted me to keep his collections of books on witchcraft and surnames and Christian names and folklore, because he knew that I would do that, I would respect somebody else's collection. But I also think that he hoped I would sell the rest and do the thing I always said I wanted to do, write a novel, because I have never written a book in my life that wasn't ordered, contracted, before I put pen to paper.

With a deadline attached.

Usually, yes, not that I have always observed it. But I knew I was going to get money for it. Except for poems in the early days, I would never write anything that I didn't know I would be paid for, and that is why I have never written a novel and that I suppose is the biggest failure of my life. I ought to have written a novel and now I don't even know if I could have written one. One short story, that was all, and even that was downgraded in the title.

What was the title?

Well, I called it *Ain't Half a Bloody Game*, but they called it *Ain't Half a Bloomin Game*. It was Harrison's great remark, Leo Harrison's. He had stumped somebody and the batsman had looked round with great indignation and Harrison said, 'It ain't half a bloody game, mate, is it?'

Poor old Bernard Hedges, do you remember Bernard Hedges? A Glamorgan opening batsman, he was a good player, but he couldn't get runs against Shack, Derek Shackleton.[33] It's appalling if you look through *Wisden*: Hedges

---

[33] Hampshire and England

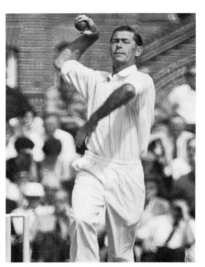

Above: Leo Harrison, 1958

Above Right: Bernard Hedges of
Glamorgan, and

Below Right: his nemesis, 'the Shack',
Derek Shackleton

caught Harrison, bowled Shackleton; and so it was again.

He turned round on this occasion, he told me – he's played
two in-duckers, and the third's an outer and he has nicked it
and Harrison's caught it – Bernard looked round and said,
'You two bs must burst out laughing every time you see me
come in.' Leo said, 'No, we don't laugh, Bernard, we are very
happy to see you.'

And he is the nicest of cricketers, and he should have
written novels himself. If I had written a novel I think it would
have been a novel about him and then, of course, it wouldn't
have been a novel at all.

This poetry and poetry reading and writing, is that personal? Which category does that fall into?

Difficult, that is the near halfway one. But the essential, I think, the one thing that has dominated my life, has been personal relationships, people. This is why I suppose I am such an appallingly sentimental person. I almost come to the end of my tether looking at *The Times* obits, because so many people I know die. When you reach this age, of course, you must expect that.

The poetry and the novels and the books informed all the rest as you have said. I just have in mind that quote from C. L. R. James that you, I think, taught me, 'What do they know of cricket who only cricket know?'

That's right, and I can remember observing at the time that in the index for that book of James's, *Beyond the Boundary*, there were more index references to T. S. Eliot than to Tony Lock.[34]

And Cardus, too, perhaps not to the same extent.

He was literary and musical. He couldn't think, he couldn't conceive, of cricket as being contained within one little ring, or one little case, or one little box, or whatever. Cricket was part of all life to him and sometimes I think, well, just how right James is. 'What do they know of cricket who only cricket know?' If you tell me somebody is cricket mad and thinks of nothing else, I don't think he is getting the fun out of it he ought to, and you don't, do you?

What, get the fun out of it?! No, seriously, I don't think only cricket matters, and I have always needed to get away from it as well as be involved in it.

---

[34] Surrey and England

C L R James at home in Brixton, London, 1986

I have always wanted to ask you, do you think that those years you took away from cricket altogether might have been the crucial years and might have made you a finer player?

You mean if I had played cricket in those years?

Yes.

I am sure I would have been a better batsman.

You probably wouldn't have been a better captain, would you?

Maybe not, it's difficult to tell about that. But I am sure I would have been a better batsman because I didn't play for England until I was 34 and I really didn't start to have a technique that I could rely on until I was well over 30. If I had had that at 25, say, or 26, it would have been six more years to improve in.

On the other hand, I suppose you are the only England

captain who has qualified in both psycho-analysis and philosophy, which must have been a help.

Well, it's an interesting question: which helped most? Did the captaining of the cricket team help the other side or the other way round? They certainly both influenced each other, in ways that are hard to put your finger on, especially the philosophy.

It must have been difficult at times after a bad day when you had gone back and wondered whether to blow your brains out or to philosophise the worry away.

Well, rationalise it away . . . yes! But why did you stop? How long did you write poetry for?

1942, or until Jack Hobbs was 70. He would have been 100 last year and that was 1982, thirty off that, 1952. Until 1952, and I tried to write a piece of verse for his seventieth birthday, and Alan Ross said, when you have finished it, send it in and I'll put it in this anthology of mine. There was one verse in the middle I couldn't get right and he rang me up. I am sure he thought I was being awkward, but it took me three months to get that one verse right. I had finished it and sent it off to him and I looked at the copy of it and I thought, that is not a very good poem and it took a long time, it stopped me often earning my living in other ways, and it's the best I can ever do.

And looking back on it, I didn't write all that many, about forty or fifty poems at the most, and it was in fact the best I had ever done. I don't think I could have done better, it said so much of what I wanted to say.

Brearley defies the Australians, Third Test, Melbourne, 1980

Would you read it for me?

Yes, surely.

To John Berry Hobbs
on his Seventieth Birthday

16 December 1952

There falls across this one December day
The light remembered from those suns of June,
That you reflected in the summer play
Of perfect strokes across the afternoon.

No yeoman ever walked his household land
More sure of step or more secure of lease
Than you, accustomed and unhurried, trod
Your small yet mighty manor of the crease.

The game the Wealden rustics handed down,
Through growing skill became, in you, a part
Of sense, and ripened to a style that showed
Their country sport matured to balanced art.

There was a wisdom so informed your bat
To understanding of the bowler's trade
That each resource of strength or skill he used
Seemed but the context of the stroke you played.

The Master: records prove the title good:
Yet figures fail you, they cannot say
How many men whose names you never knew
Were proud to tell their sons they saw you play.

They share the sunlight of your summer day
Of thirty years; and they, with you, recall
How, through those well-wrought centuries, your hand
Reshaped the history of bat and ball.

Jack Hobbs

It was a little birthday present. He wrote and said, 'How very nice. I know nothing about poetry, but because you wrote it it must be good.' That was the sort of splendid thing he used to say.

The great Jack Hobbs, 1930

The essential thing about Jack was his humility. He was determined to be content. He was the oldest of eleven children of a rather poor man. And his great fun was to go to church. He used to go to church two, three times on Sunday, perhaps to an Evangelist church and to the Church of England. He loved going to church services and I think he did absorb much of the gospel and try desperately hard to live up to it. Where you go from that, or if you could have gone from that into the present day, I am not sure. There was a certain saintliness about this man that perhaps wouldn't sort well with the present day.

On the other hand, you see, he wasn't a milk-and-water type. He was an inveterate practical joker. You got up to leave him and he'd say, 'Oh, Jack, would you like that, that, that?' And he'd give you back two fountain-pens, a propelling pencil and your wallet, which he had picked out of your pocket without your knowing. And he used to do this thing at the Oval, where he'd synchronise a few players. Perhaps one of the men who was just due in would be writing a letter in the corner of the dressing-room. Then Jack would synchronise them and up would go the six of them and say 'That's it, he's out, pal. Oh dear, oh dear, oh dear.' This chap would drop his pen, grab his bat and gloves and three times Jack got them halfway down the steps in the Oval Gentlemen vs. Players match, before the chap realised the batsman was still there. A good joker with a very positive sense of humour. But without malice.

I did meet him once, actually. My first cricket bat was signed by Jack Hobbs. My father took me down to his shop and he signed it for me, and I remember exactly what the bat looked like and what his signature looked like. I was 9 or 10.

Yes. Now, do you know, even that autograph was a bit hard, because if you can remember the signature, it was a painful, cramped hand. He didn't write easily and he used sometimes to say to me, 'Jack, I have had a lot of letters on my birthday [or on a knighthood or something like that], could you frame a reply for me?' And a couple of times I said, 'Well, look, it's so easy, I'll get it duplicated for you and you just sign it.'

'No, no,' he would say, 'if people write to me they expect me to write back to them.' And he said, 'If you compose the letter and send it to me, it will be shorter than if I do it.' But for instance, I reckon he was still writing acknowledgement or thank-you letters six months afterwards, a ration of them every day, in this rather painful hand, and he never let anybody think they were a nuisance.

He almost belonged to a different age. The second time that Arthur Mailey bowled him with a slow full toss in a Test Match, they both threw back their heads and laughed. I just don't see it happening today, do you?

No, no, I don't.

Jack Hobbs, 1935

And Wilfred Rhodes once said, 'How many hundreds did Jack make, 197? Aye,' he said, 'he could have made it 297 if he wanted.' He certainly did at times absolutely give it away.

He used to say, 'You see, if Sandy and I have got about 70 or 80 by half-past twelve, or a quarter-to-one, there are a lot of good batsman to come, you know – Tom Barling,[35] Andy Ducat,[36] Mr Fender, Mr Jardine – a lot of good players.' So you pick on one of your old pals, tell him to put a couple of men deep, have a swing and get out for about 70.'

But of course when you weren't doing so well, that was the time when you had to earn your money and put your head down and get some runs. He had a great, again almost feudal, sense of this. If you consider he had to go through all the qualification period, come down from Cambridge, live in London lodgings all the winter – and they used from time to time to call up the lodgings to see that he was really qualifying by residence. It was a different world in every way, cricket and everything else.

As we were saying just now, it did tend to be a very feudal game. I always remember Jack Hobbs, simply not wanting captaincy. They had to press him very hard when he took over

[35] Surrey
[36] Surrey and England

from . . . was it Arthur Carr when he was injured? Until his dying day, Jack referred to the amateurs as Mr, even though he himself was Sir Jack.

I said to him, 'If only you had had the business earlier, you could have played as an amateur.' 'Oh, I wouldn't have wanted to. I was very content to be a professional, I didn't want to be an amateur.' Indeed, sometimes Jack seemed almost too good to be true. But you see this rang true right through his life. I have never found a flaw and I have asked one or two pretty hard characters, not other county cricketers but people who have had to do with him, and they found the same idealistic streak.

One thing that was striking about him was this terrific conscientiousness and steadiness and gentleness. Was he gentle?

He was incredibly gentle. He really was devoted, you know, to his children and above all to his wife. He nursed his wife as tenderly as a woman for the last four or five years of her life and bore everything with patience. When she died it was as if he said, now it's all right; he just slid out of this life.

He just was the person whom I suppose I admired more than anybody else and I really believe that if he had never played cricket I would have admired him as much. He was a very, very fine human being. Of course a fine human being like that doesn't make a very good book. I could only write a book about a good man, and books about good men I don't think people want to read nowadays.

Are you saying you were not happy with that book?

Oh, I was completely happy with it. It might have been fuller, it might have been bigger, but it says what I want it to say, and you can only go on continuing the parade of great innings that he played. But sometimes I used to think that he was nearer perfection than anybody else that ever played.

He could joke, you see. Arthur Mailey told this story about getting him on a dusty one once and bowling a big leg-break. Jack went across the stumps and hit it against the spin through square-leg, and said in that strange croaky voice of his ,'Ah, poor old Arthur, they always put you on when the ball won't turn.' This leg-break had done about a foot! And he used to chip, you know, he used to chip over the fieldsman's head. He could do wonderful things with a cricket bat.

You said that you could wish that you had written a novel. What is the best thing that you wrote?

I don't think there is much doubt about it – *Fred*, the biography of Fred Truman.

It's come out in a new edition recently with a new chapter, hasn't it?

A chapter on Fred's after-life!

I am sure it will be a success again. And on the subject of regret, in all the pressure of work and writing to deadlines and writing commissioned books, do you feel that you might have spent longer over something and done something that was even better?

I don't think so. I am a 'putter-offer' of work by nature. I have to get up and attack it because it's got to be done. No, poetry was the writing for fun most of my life. I mean, when I would write on spec and without hope or expectation of payment. But I am a professional writer and I enjoy being a professional writer. There are many things I couldn't be bothered to write about, that didn't interest me. I have written about the things that interested me, with infinite pleasure.

Jim Swanton told me that he asked you if you would help him with The Cricketer *when he was editor of it and it had no money and there was very little it could pay. He said that he asked you to do articles regularly, with him suggesting topics, and he said you never said no and you never, ever, gave the copy in late. That is very much part of being a professional, isn't it?*

I think so, yes. Yes, that was a tough effort; it kept *The Cricketer* afloat.

John Arlott in the commentary box with Fred Truman during Fred's 'afterlife',
Prudential World Cup, 1979

In a sense this is a sort of verbal autobiography. Have you ever thought of writing an autobiography?

I have thought of it and I have been tempted because the offers of advances have been very big, but I don't like writing in the first person. It's different on an occasion like this if you are answering questions, but as a general rule I don't like first-person-singular writing. I think I can say, in the last ten years, the word 'I' has only twice appeared in my copy and on each occasion it was written in by a sub-editor.

That's remarkable really. Has it been self-denial?

No, it's been a discipline, and if I wrote an autobiography I would want to try and write it without the use of the first person singular. I think it would be a great help if somebody wrote an autobiography by standing back and referring to themselves in the third person. I think you would come far nearer the truth if you did that.

Does the prospect of dying frighten you?

139

Not any more, no. My son Jim has gone, my second wife Valerie has gone, my little girl has gone, my mother has gone, my father has gone. I am not frightened to go where they are. I am hard on three score years and ten. I have had a wonderful time and I think of my contemporaries who have gone, those killed in the war.

I remember George Brown who played for Hampshire, an all-rounder of all all-rounders. I left his son, young George, in the police courtyard one night in Southampton. I said, 'Where are you going, George?' He said, 'I have got to take the Chief Constable up to Basset.' I said, 'That's lucky, I am going to headquarters,' and I turned and walked into headquarters. He got into the car to go and collect the Chief Constable and got the next stick of bombs. You see, it's your card that's marked, or the one that's got your number.

John Arlott

You have talked to me about how not death, but the idea of becoming helpless in old age, is something that really terrifies you and you are determined not to suffer.

That's right. I remember reading the definition of the people in mental hospitals: 'Reduced to the stature of a normal healthy vegetable.' That is what I couldn't bear. I don't mind dying, but by heaven I want to die with some dignity. Struck by lightning perhaps – for a second time!

You did some work for Age Concern, didn't you?

Yes, I did, and I am sure that there is so much that one can do for the elderly to help them. You see, all you have to do is help them to realise that they are not hopelessly old, and then the whole thing is saved.

I am nearly 70 and I work as hard as ever I have worked in my life, I really do. I don't dislike it. All right, I am lucky, I am working at the things I like doing. Sometimes when I get really tied up with something, my wife says, 'Come in for your dinner. Why don't you stop?' But I would sooner carry on than have my dinner, sometimes. I don't like to dig the garden very much. There are all sorts of work that I don't count, but there is a lot of work that keeps me alive. Without it I would just go.

John, thank you very much indeed for agreeing to spend the time to do this programme. It has been very enjoyable for me to talk to you and listen to you.

You know it's always been a pleasure for me to talk to you, so it's mutual.

Can I just ask you a last question? You have come to Alderney. You have got off the mainland and you are cut off, not completely, but you are cut off from a lot of your work. Yet as we have discussed, you are still extremely busy; you have lots of projects. What do you hope to achieve now? What would you like to do?

I would like to go on writing to the same standard of competence for the rest of my days, until I die, and I would like to die with dignity.

Thank you.

ILLUSTRATION CREDITS